MULBERRY TROUT

MULBERRY TROUT

or The Delights of Dry Fly Fishing
A Collection of Fishing Stories

by
OGDEN BIGELOW

with illustrations by
LEE BART

CHARLES E. TUTTLE CO.: PUBLISHERS
Rutland, Vermont

Representatives
Continental Europe: Boxerbooks, Inc., Zurich
British Isles: Prentice-hall International, Inc., London
Australasia: Paul Flesch & Co., Pty. Ltd., Melbourne
Canada: M.G. Hurtig Ltd., Edmonton

Published by the Charles E. Tuttle Company, Inc.
of Rutland, Vermont & Tokyo, Japan
with editorial offices at
Suido 1-chome, 2-6, Bunkyo-ku, Tokyo, Japan

First edition 1969
Second printing, 1970

Book Plan by Roland A. Mulhauser
Library of Congress Catalog Card No. 69-16177
Standard Book No. 8048-0194-0

Printed in Japan

To my wife—who doesn't fish—
but understands

CONTENTS

ILLUSTRATIONS *11*

PREFACE *13*

THE CATSKILLS *15*

The Catskills and the Early Years
Here Today and Gone Tomorrow
Mother Nature—April 1948
The Last Fish
Does Courtesy Pay Off?
The Solution
Skill and Brains
The Bigelow Pool
Fishing with the Distaff
Artistic Dunking

THE EAST *65*

The East, or the Learning Process
Four of a Kind
The Boy Next Door
Naming a Fly
Piscatorial and Other Genealogy

CONTENTS

The Three Graces
Good Luck Only
The Jumper Proves the Rule
Frustration
The Light Still Flickers in the Window

THE WEST *111*

The West
The Eton Collar
Bugaboo
We Live and Learn —First Lesson (A.M.)
We Live and Learn—Second Lesson (P.M.)
'Legal Trout'
Reading the Bottom

ABROAD *145*

Fields Abroad, or The Declining Years
By-Products
The First Grandchild
The Second Grandchild
The Measure of the Fish, or Bombs Away
The Tombstone Touch
Chile
The Test
Fecundity

CONTENTS

OTHER FISH *197*

Other Fish, A Postscript
Smelt
Large-Mouth Bass
Great Northern Pike
Small-Mouth Bass
Atlantic Salmon

ICHTHYBIGELOGICAL RESEARCH
OR
THOUGHTFUL MOMENTS

Salmo Irideus Brown
Was a banker of some renown
But when he took up fishin'
He went to perdition
And now he's a bum—on the town.

Salmo Fario Hertz
Was a banker—who got his deserts
The inside of his hide
With Bourbon he plied
So now, when you squeeze him, he squirts!

A girl in the bank named Alice
Was so anxious to eat Fontinalis
That her boss—Salvelinus
Oh "strictly between us"
*Set her up by the stream—in a palace.**

* A case of a banker going for bust.

ILLUSTRATIONS

Here Today and Gone Tomorrow 21
Mother Nature 27
The Last Fish 31
The Bigelow Pool 47
Fishing with the Distaff Side 57
Artistic Dunking 61
The East, or The Learning Process 69
Naming a Fly 80
Piscatorial and Other Genealogy 85
The Light Still Flickers in the Window 109
The Eton Collar 117
Legal Trout 135
Reading the Bottom 143
By-Products 154
The First Grandchild 159
The Tombstone Touch 175
Chile 183
Smelt 202
Small-Mouth Bass 208

PREFACE

NEVER HAVING WRITTEN A BOOK, there were many things I had to learn the hard way. Among them was that my favorite title would not attract the largest group of potential customers. Readers seem harder to catch than trout. Maybe I can hide it somewhere for those other evil souls who read carefully. Many stupid titles occurred and there was one suggested which even I would not dare present to any publisher. There are so many books about trout that there just plain had to be a title other than the banalities.

Frankly I hope *Mulberry Trout* will cause a little curiosity, that you bought the book for that reason, and that you enjoy some of my discomfortures if nothing else. The name *Mulberry Trout,* so far as I know, is my own invention. I didn't find it in an ichthyological dictionary, it came from the nursery rhyme, "All Around the Mulberry Bush the Banker Chased the Trout." Also mulberry wine can be good!

I have found that mulberry bushes flourish best in the immediate vicinity of good trout streams. This seems to be universally true whether in the eastern or western United States, or outside this country. Mulberry trout have been caught by millions of fishermen and their nicknames could be "Brookie," "Brownie," "Rainbow," "Cut Throat," "Dolly Varden," and others. Does that splake for itself?

It is also obvious to me that Mulberry bushes grow best on

the food of friendship, in fact once started, they grow like fish stories. I think of the bush, the monkey, and the weasel as well as all those nice people, including my family, who have become the background for my very own particular Mulberry Bush. For these and other reasons I have divided this book into five sections which happen to fall into overlapping periods of my own trout fishing experiences of more than forty years. Maybe this will help a few to guess what I am dreaming about.

So I've tickled my memories and put some of them on paper. It's been done largely for my own amusement and perhaps in part because of the satisfaction of fishing, good company and good times. Some friends have died; the infirmities of age have limited others to conversation only; and still others, I'm ashamed to admit, have taken up less worthy avocations. In spite of this, I miss them also. I've always hated to fish alone. I don't mean I have to have a companion in my lap, but I do like a friend on a stream—say a quarter mile away. A sandwich on the stream could not taste better than with a friend. At the end of the day, some spoofing mixed with the serious, or just recounting little observations can be as good for the soul, and the next trip, as a limit day.

Analyses, speeches, reports of many shapes and sizes have helped increase my pension and would have reduced my years had it not been for fishing. Maybe I'm trying to create a phantom friend for the years ahead. Maybe you can share my sandwich and chuckle mildly either at or with me. I hope so.

THE CATSKILLS

The Catskills and the Early Years

THEY ARE BEAUTIFUL but in recent years have been characterized for me by too many small hatchery trout and unhatched people. For the good of your soul however, you should lookup John Burroughs *Locusts and Wild Honey* and read his description of trout fishing on the Esopus in the last century. This will restore your faith and paint real beauty.

In the early years, you go fishing to catch fish. I started in the Catskills because I could reach them of a Friday evening and get back to the office by nine for Monday morning work. This was important to a youngster who then could find inexpensive accommodations; who was willing to wade wet April 1st in sneakers and whose budget and job consciousness limited him to so many weekends a year. It must also be admitted that digging worms or changing flies was more fun than changing diapers. My wife was patient and I let off steam by fishing the East Branch of the Delaware, Dry Brook, the Ellenville Stream, the Willowemoc, the Esopus, occasionally the Beaverkill and most of all, my beloved Schoharie Creek. Here I found good food, good accommodations and good trout, if you worked hard. I also made many many friends.

So I have gone back, and still do, to refresh old memories and re-examine certain spots that I have studied for years, and always in the hope of meeting old friends. After all, when you have reached the age of retirement from active business, the number or size of the fish you keep are not as important as the many interesting things you see and hear. For that matter, now that you are able to take a week or two if you want to, it is still refreshing to re-live the anticipation of a weekend instead of just buying a safari.

Here Today & Gone Tomorrow

IN THE MID-THIRTIES, I was young enough to go fishing in the Catskills on April 1st, come hell or high water. Both usually came. However I had survived the depression and acquired sense and money enough to buy waders, instead of fishing wet, as in preceding years. My exuberance and that of my friends was greater than that of the frozen fish we caught. We really fished from dawn 'til dark. Keeping the line in the water helped overcome lack of skill. A modest supply of Applejack generally stayed in the back pocket. It could restore life when really necessary. This avoided interrupting the fishing because of rigor mortis.

Fewer people in those days talked about the number of fish they released—certainly not those in my age group. We wanted fish! Garden hackle, fished carefully seemed to best match high, cold and muddy water. I say we fished carefully, with due respect, for to fish a worm well is no easier in my opinion than to fish a dry or wet fly. While I now prefer the dry fly and warmer waters, I am satisfied that much of what knowledge I have acquired came this hard way. I have since then caught trout on a dry fly in a snowstorm. All of which proves that Lady Luck should never be slighted, and that fishermen stop at nothing.

Other things are different also. In those days, ambitious youngsters did not readily take a day off. Saturday work was a part of the accepted order of things and jobs were something to be valued. Saturday was only a half day however, and, if not taken too often, one could do a fair job of rationalizing. A weekend of fishing was something to be treasured. An early supper Friday was cheaper at home. A long drive afterwards did not bother either youthful blood or madness. The first weekend was real luxury and almost satisfied the soul for two whole weeks.

One such jaunt started with a Friday midnight arrival on the Ellenville Stream. The reward Saturday was two small trout, legal, both six inches! The reward for the soul came at supper and was the story of an eleven pound Brownie.

Off we went to the hardware store where the fish and half the local population were on display. The story was true, a big male, undershot jaw and all. He must have been living on trout twice the size of mine, because mine couldn't possibly provide the necessary nourishment.

"Joe caught him on a worm. Going to get him mounted. Took the worm at daylight in the big pool below the bridge."

There'd be no hope of fishing there Sunday. No other fish could move because of the fishermen. Every man in the hardware store asked, "Did he fight?" Fishermen are sometimes sensible, but not always. Tackle? Well, it wasn't a willow and a bent pin, but he wasn't captured on a 4X leader either! Two buttons had popped from the chest of the captor. It took me about thirty years to lose one button. That night a mild sedative from Sunday's supply of Applejack. Physical fatigue and mental exhaustion permitted no dreams.

Sunday morning was another day and more hard fishing and even better luck than Saturday's two fish. I caught two more a small fraction over six inches. I was coming up in the world! Going downstream that afternoon, I found a tree across most of the stream and really messing up a deep, narrow pool. Could I get a hook and a worm under the tree or at least under

most of the branches? There was only one way to find out. I knew there were fish there. There had to be! In the second hour, with some adjustment of a split shot and my position upstream, I found I could. It had its reward! I could feel a fish taking! Was it a trout or a sucker? Patience, my boy, patience. Wait! Raise the tip! He's there! Strike but not too hard! This is trout! He's better than Saturday's two or this morning's two either. Unfortunately I knew and felt in my bones, hand and mind that he would not match the hardware store job, but I could and did work him out of the tree. Ten and one half inches is at least four inches better than any fish I had. This was a psychological victory! Hereafter I should always fish the tree tops.

It wasn't all just fishing however, for in those days the artist in us required that we search out enough ferns or grass to make a pleasant bed in the creel. My giant had to be cleaned and bedded down with his friends before dark. Creeds seem to change.

Sunday night I arrived home after eleven. I let myself in quietly. After my coat and tackle, were parked in the entryway, I headed for the kitchen with my creel. Passing the stairway, a stage whisper said, "Daddy"! It was my eight year old daughter in her nightie at the head of the stairs.

"Yes, Winkie. What are you doing up at this hour?"

"Did you catch any fish?"

"Yes, Winkie, five."

"May I see them?"

"Yes, Winkie, if you go right to sleep."

So she admired the fish—all of them including "the great big one." My vanity was recovering. I paddled her behind lightly and we both went to bed.

In the morning when I came to breakfast I had my real surprise. This little tyke had managed to get up first, cook, and eat all five trout!

Now what would you do but love her!

Mother Nature—April 1948

MORE SENTIMENTAL STORIES have been written about father and son "taking to the wild" than there are authors. Problems of the parents maturity, studies, economics and world problems are settled this way, usually with emotion, good advice to all hands and at least one moral principle clearly delineated. Clarity comes out of chaos; pain is eliminated. Confusion lives no longer and both father and son live happily ever after. They both ultimately bathe in mutual admiration and some author writes another story which also turns out perfectly. The sun bursts through cloudy skies, some son.

Most boys have problems. They increase with the years. All fathers have problems; they also increase with the years. Most sons seem to love their fathers. Most fathers love their sons, or think they do. Many fathers try to live their sons lives for them. How long they keep trying depends on both father and son. When fathers reach the point where they can no longer tell the boy, and get away with it, they resort to indirection, which after all is what the boy did with the first or second first class yowl from the crib. Really, the kids are pretty good at finagling. They catch on fast! Maybe if they think the old man is really clever they will play along with him.

Now I love the outdoors and I see it best through a fisherman's eyes. I hoped my son would do likewise, but I knew that the direct approach wouldn't work. I also knew that at that time he was keenly interested in photography, so one early spring I carefully set up a weekend where he could photograph in color those first leaves "the size of a squirrel's ear," where the first red buds and the first light green of the willows would respond to his artistry and where the sunset at the Bigelow pool could be perpetually preserved in memory of our weekend together.

He accepted with alacrity, though perhaps with a motorcycle in mind. His old man, blissfully unconscious of everything except his own scheming, proceeded to plot his son's downfall. The first day the old man fell in. That added a mild amount of hilarity. We took pictures of the sunset, the red buds, etc., etc., etc. Pop was in the groove. It was carefully worked out that mine host, a marvelous fisherman, joined us the second day in fishing a small tributary stream. Somehow he seemed to take charge. He raised the question with my son, "How would you like to show up your old man?" off they went together in fine spirit, and took the best pocket water completely out of my hands. This was fine with me. Everything was going according to plan. So I rested the water, waited until they were well out of sight, secretly wished them both success, and proceeded to fish myself without great effort.

Wouldn't it be wonderful if the boy really got bitten by the trout bug! I was all prepared to be lost in admiration. I was even prepared, in case the fishing got too good, to put my fish back! There was nothing quite so important as that my son should do better than I. I ached to cheer for him.

Actually the fishing was pretty good and I did put a few fish back, just day dreaming and thinking of the years to come when we could visit the wilds together and take the biggest fish extant.

Time passed, and in due course I'd fished through a beautiful stand of pines and was well into a long open stretch where the wind blew and I noticed for the first time it had started to sleet. It was getting more and more chilly and so was I. Right in the middle of the "wide open spaces" I met them hurrying back to the car. They had their limit, both of them. I slobbered congratulations all over everything. My hopes were being realized, but as I went into my act, my son showed great impatience to get down out of the wind and into the pines, particularly when it started to hail. At that point I did too, but with neither his speed or enthusiasm.

It really hailed! To say billiard balls would be a slight exaggeration but those marbles, when they came down and hit bare knuckles, they bounced! The other few million that hit the ground also bounced. A white one in the back of the neck left a pink spot. Maybe that's what made me think of billiard balls.

My son was really in a hurry and the harder it hailed the more we all hurried. Old legs could not keep up with young ones too well. The ground was getting whiter and our knuckles were turning black and blue! Our necks had gone from pink to red! Thank heavens my hat had a crown! We finally got there and the old man sounded like Engine 99 letting off steam. Praise be for the "sheltering pines"! The boy was still in high gear and with some comment about "mother nature" kept on into the bushes.

We waited and shivered. He didn't return. Poppa went looking for his baby boy. As I got into the brush, I heard muffled comment and distinctly unfriendly noises of some sort. Another comment! Another kind of noise! Emphatic comment! More noise. I paused to listen and became concerned. It finally dawned that my son was really mad! This was nothing, absolutely nothing like anything I'd ever heard from my darling boy before! I acquired a certain respect for his language at this early age.

Summoning my courage, I rushed through the brambles and

there he stood, all alone if not soundless, and with his waders around his ankles! His back was to me. I called, "What's the matter?"

Something was said about some breeze—and then, "My hands are so damned sore and cold I can't pull up my zipper!"

Now in a situation like this, a graven image might smile even though every parental rule forbids laughter at the plight of the progeny! I gave in. The direction of his classical comment swiveled from zipper to parent. I bent over, and fell down, and started to laugh some more. That was when I asked for his camera! For awhile it looked as if I might remain there—trampled to death! He was old enough and strong enough to do it! Taking to the wild had turned him that way!

"You think this is funny!"

"I know darned well it's funny!"

"I can't go back this way!"

"You sure can if you pull up your waders. Do you need help on that too?"

"Shut up!"

I got to my feet, we got in the car, and went back to the inn. When we got there, the brogues came off according to rule. We padded inside, waders and all. There were ladies present. He was committed to silence by a slow burn and his old man by physical fear. Conversation would certainly have raised more questions than silence.

The waders helped the thawing process. We still didn't look at each other. I was beginning to sweat but was still somewhat cowed. Finally he broke the ice, "Pop, these waders are colder than the weather outside! Let's go out and change." He insisted on changing in the barn. Both the hands and zipper worked! We returned to the bar, friends again in spite of a limit catch, dirty looks and "the wide open spaces."

This was twenty years ago. We both laugh now. There's nothing like "a family bond by zipper." I haven't fished in

MOTHER NATURE—APRIL 1948

April since then. He hasn't fished these twenty years. He says trout fishing is too dangerous. He skis. All of which goes to show that when father and son "take to the wild" you never know what the hell will happen!

The Last Fish

THE SUMMER HAD BEEN DRY and discouraging. The trips had been a little more infrequent than usual and a little more discouraging. But September came and it was the first year that the great State of New York permitted trout fishing up until September 30th.

I took the last week in September and found it refreshing as always, more beautiful than usual with the turning leaves. The days were getting shorter and inevitably the last day arrived. Thinking of the season practically behind me, I started early with a small lunch and large hopes.

The day had its rewards and I found that when the fish come this late they have made most of their transition from hatchery to a properly ordained life. Their flesh is firm and their actions, when they act, are incisive.

Over the course of the day I had caught a few "keepers" to take home to friends, who seemed to appreciate both the fish and myself. I had also been alone and fished all day in a leisurely manner. The great hurrah crowds of spring were absent. The water had just as much sparkle as ever and the leaves were not quite proclaiming winter by falling in the stream. No hatch of flies was apparent. Each cast was made with the bottom in mind. There was no "fishing the rise."

It had been a satisfying day and when dusk neared I had no regrets and started back to the inn a little early. I had to pass the "Tool House" pool. This was the spot dedicated by the hatchery to the boys of today, and as a by-product to the meat hunters of today also. A small stream entered the large one; there was a deep pool with an eddy and a high gravel bank on the near side, created no doubt by the spring freshets.

In the spring and early summer no self-respecting dry fly man would show up there for fear of getting tangled in somebody's worms, spinners, spoons or hair, but it is still a beautiful pool. The workmen at the Tool House had gone home and out of sheer sentiment, I drove my car in and parked.

Did you ever just stand and watch the water, trying to make up your mind whether or not you'd fish? My mind was made up for me. I saw a good swirl. This meant scrambling down a ten foot bank, assisted by roots polished by numerous men and boys. I made it! I also made it across the tributary stream, and again the fish rose. He didn't come out of water. I couldn't see what, if anything, he was feeding on. Maybe he was just thinking, like I was, of the trials and tribulations of the preceding summer. The question was, what to do about it, followed immediately by the second question, how? He would be hard to reach but he would be worth it.

My back cast couldn't go out behind because the bank was well above my head. I had to get a long line across and slightly down the pool but with reasonably good float potentials. Not all my casts were perfect. Some of them were normal. Experience has taught me to periodically check the barb. It was fortunate that I did. The light was failing and I was barely able to put on a new fly. The fish was still coming. He did not take my ten or a dozen offerings. There wasn't time to change the fly again, at least for my eyes there wasn't. So I tried again. This time he took, I lifted my rod and was into a good fish!

Up and down that pool from one side to the other, back and forth he went. I couldn't see him now but I could feel every fin whether he was deep or on the surface. I did keep a tight line.

I didn't see the fish. I could feel him tiring. I knew I was getting somewhere.

The bank behind me sloped sharply into deep water. I got out to about my knees on the slope. I didn't dare go farther because I couldn't see and besides, the fish was tiring. I unslipped my net. I was able to hold that fish with one hand. My net was in the water and for the first time I could see a vague outline of what I thought was the best trout I had ever hooked on this stream.

My knees bent. I gained another foot or two of line and was ready for the last fish. He was coming in. His tail splashed. The line went slack! The hook had pulled out. The big fish gets away, but you keep him forever.

Does Courtesy Pay Off?

AUGUST IN THE CATSKILLS can be warm, very warm, or very damned hot. The streams can be low, very low, or almost not. Fishermen can be bored, stubbornly persistent, stupid or, conceivably, highly skilled. If they fish in the heat of the day, they are apt to cover the first three characterizations completely, and they so characterized me one hot leveling afternoon. I had a blind urge to utilize a few available hours in the hope the subconscious mind could come up with something useful. There wasn't any justified hope for fish, but the old exception-that-proves-the-rule did get a wry reward.

It was the middle of the week and the temptation to put a rod in the car, in case a business date didn't last too long, was much too much for a weekend fisherman. What difference would it really make whether I got any fish, whether I got back to the bank at five, or home at midnight? Knowing my soul needed something, or at least that I did, or maybe I just wanted to play hooky, I had a unique day: home late enough to avoid the bank, early enough to raid the icebox, and amused enough to chuckle for a long long time.

My business was probably hurried. The car found its way up the old dirt road. It was carefully parked in the shade, heading out. I checked the road up stream and changed my pants. Another check and I was comfortably shirted. This was a day when old bones could wade wet and even enjoy it afterwards. That greasy old friend, my fishing vest, was hot, but maybe I'd fall in. This was high and lazy adventure.

The fishing was as expected. It soon became certain that better casting than I could produce, a very long leader, and pools with less gin, were the only hope for anything beyond a possible lethargic hatchery fish of small proportions, physically and mentally. However, I persisted. There wasn't any evidence of anyone else who could catch me in the act of losing my senses. My emotions were being satisfied. If I could snag just one good fish I'd be a hero in my own eyes. It was dead quiet—no breeze, no movement I could see, no fishermen and particularly none of the mad meat hunters of May and June throwing boulders in their consuming haste. Think of it, no bank, no telephone, no nothing.

But something was in ambush. There never was a dry fly man yet who did not sooner or later get to the "around the bend" part. Here we are. I, too, came "around the bend" and found a pool—and another fisherman! He was well up in the pool and obviously intent on his job. He hadn't heard me and I took pains that he shouldn't. So much good fishing or just plain pleasure has been spoiled by brash or inconsiderate acts. We could all give chapter and verse. I sat on a boulder and watched. Courtesy might pay off.

It soon became apparent, even from a distance, that while I might share some of his thoughts, I was certainly not blessed with his skill. He was a master, and any experienced man could see it. The effortless grace of his back cast was a joy to watch. Even if I couldn't see the fly light, I knew it must be generally perfect. Two fish were either rising or dimpling for he always cast to one of two locations. His hat looked comfortable—no aurora borialis. His clothes showed no stain from any emporium of piscatorial profit—easy and well used. All in all it was a satisfying performance to watch. In about ten minutes he hooked his fish. Without hurry or loss of poise, his sure touch brought it away from its neighbor. Never once did he have to look down stream to where I sat.

In due course a decent fish was netted, examined and put away. I'm glad I stifled the impulse to walk up and congratulate him. It seemed pleasanter to watch him dry his fly, light a cigarette, rest the pool briefly and start after the other fish.

He'd caught a good fish and I'd learned several lessons, reflected mightly and reached the conclusion that the decent thing to do was to leave him alone. This decision took thought and effort. Here was the kind of a guy I'd really like to talk with. I was sure I'd respect him as well as his skill. I also hoped he'd respect me. If I intruded he'd probably be courteous. I wanted more than that. So I decided to go on upstream and hope he'd catch up with me later. He never did. I now regret this for two reasons, himself and the desire to ask him "Does courtesy pay off"? Maybe he got his two fish and stopped. I'll never know, unless he reads this yarn and tells me.

So my cigarette was dunked, my fly secured and I eased over to the bank quietly and headed back into the woods. Walking upstream for perhaps a quarter mile, I could think of little but emulating his lessons while still fresh in my mind. I pondered all the satisfactions of fishing. Here was a man doing the right thing with ease and without any effort. He was succeeding. Maybe I was too, for I was accomplishing my purpose of the day. I was soothing my disposition—passing the buck to my subconscious mind—and calming my soul.

This was so until I cut over toward the stream again. Then I heard voices which increased in number and became louder as I neared the stream. Fishing was definitely over for the day. The pool was full of forty or fifty men and women—all stark naked!

Problems—there are always problems! How does one fish for forty or fifty men and women? What size hook? Where should it be placed? Wet? Dry? Obviously wet outside. Dry inside, open to question. Here I really learned that the biggest fish is not always the most attractive—for example a big male with an undershot jaw and belly. Who'd want him? Light tackle—heavy tackle or a rod of iron? Nylon or gut leader? There was too much natural gut already. Did one want the limit or just a couple to take home? Or could I take a choice one home? Or are there any choice ones? What sort of a creel or bassinet would you put those babies in? Was the limit poundage or number? Was I after wild fish or freshly stocked ones? What was I after? What should I be after?

Spellbound I stood among the trees and watched these lethargic denizens of aqua something or other flop around. Some were huge. Some made great swirls under the water and others on the surface. None made an arch in the air and came down on the fly (the flies were happy). None seemed to be feeding, and none seemed to be playing—they were just porpoising around.

Well stacked pool?

Does courtesy pay off?

I don't know.

What the hell!

The Solution

ONCE UPON A TIME, the railroads ran passenger coaches on branch lines to cover the vacation business, plus a few fishermen. With the war, gasoline was rationed. At the same time, those of us who had responsibilities, and were past our most useful age to the Army, were generally working ourselves to exhaustion. We were sometimes able to refresh ourselves and our viewpoints by a short weekend of fishing a few times during the season. This was the onc thing most refreshing to us and sometimes enabled us to pick up the pressure again.

New orthodox waders were non-existent. Those filmy plastic jobs had not yet appeared. We struggled with what we had. It was under such circumstances that I started fishing one stream in the Catskills with a joy in the surroundings and in the fellows I fished with that has lasted for over a quarter century.

My host, mentor, and guide was allowed a limited amount of gasoline because fishing was his business. He never had quite enough. In consequence, you started with the group in the early morning, or you walked. You stayed on the stream for lunch, or you walked, or went without lunch. In the afternoon, you were "on the road" to be picked up at a fixed minute, or you walked. When you and the others were crammed into the car and holding great creels of fish out the window, you met the train on the way back.

If you fell into the stream, you got wet. Those with warm

hearts got dry eventually. If the day was cold, you were also. In the early season it was not always warm enough to enjoy a dunking.

If the waders leaked, you also got wet. If you didn't like being wet, you tried applying a patch. The adhesives for patches didn't work as well as they do today. The harried fisherman was not as patient. He didn't have as much time to fish. We tried to patch our waders before they were really dry. That doesn't work. We stayed up late in the evening, if we had the patience, to get the waders dry and that meant we missed some sleep. In the morning, sleepy or not, we started at the appointed hour, sometimes with the waders half on and sometimes half off, sometimes with the head half baked, and nearly always with the patches half stuck.

If the patches had not stuck, you either fished with the leak or walked back. This was the accepted order of life. I might add, this is a hell of a way to get a bath!

The first time I arrived at the spot called the Westkill Tavern I had no knowledge of that wonderful spot nor of Art Flick, his father, his wife, or his sons. I arrived in time to see a gentleman, and I mean a gentleman, taking off his waders. He had fallen in. No water was running out. It was all held inside. The patchwork was superb! This was the thing above all else that struck you right between the eyes! The color effect was also magnificent. There were brown patches, red patches, green patches, yellow patches and some blue ones, let alone the black and white. There were long ones, there were short ones, there were round ones and I swear there were two that looked like kidneys! They appeared at the knees, the ankles, all seams, the front and, of course, a big one on the seat. The arrangement of colors was charming, but nowhere near the smile of the occupant which rose out of this wet miasma.

"Do they leak?"

"No."

"Did you fall in?"

"Yes."

"You got wet."

"Your observations are very acute."

"Were you fishing Greenwell's Glory?"

"No, and it wasn't a female Beaverkill either. Look, here's what I was fishing. Here's one for you. Now you go to the Judge's Pool, go below it. There's a big slippery rock. Don't stand on it unless you want to do what I did. Fish a long line from above. There's a good fish there. I have to leave in the morning."

I had never met the guy before and had never fished the stream before. Over the last quarter century I met him many times. He could always unscramble trouble. You always, after a few minutes, got the feeling that here was the grandest guy to fish with that ever existed, and that you were the next on the list.

I felt it then. I didn't get the big fish, but I did meet a genius of sorts.

The next year I met him again. He was dry. He had some fish. He had the same smile and the next morning, when we dressed for the stream he had new waders!

"Look here Tony, where did you get those waders? Who did you bribe? What did they cost? How did you find them? Is there another pair?"

Tony grinned for quite awhile. Not only his eyes and his mouth, but even his waders grinned. Finally, "Ogden, you definitely couldn't get away with it."

"Why?"

"I impersonated a Baptist Minister."

Skill and Brains

ALL OF US, EVEN "WEEKENDERS", secretly admit to ourselves that we know something about trout fishing. The better the fisherman, the less he talks about it—but the gentleman has other ways of satisfying his ego. Very often the other fellow can be sorted out simply by allowing him to do the talking. Ever try it? I'm willing to wager if you've been around as long as I have, you've also observed others appraising you. If they are clumsy, don't you feel a bit superior? And if their approach is up to your standards, don't you warm up a bit? Under such circumstances, can't you recall various fish when pride in your skill and brains produced a prize particularly worthy of yourself? Of course you have—and so have I—frequently!

Also, the cult that assures that we men have more brains than trout, is increasing. Some writers have even had the temerity to point out that trout are not necessarily wily, lightning brained, equipped with the wisdom of Solomon, or connoisseurs of color, hackles and size of hook. They even point out that our admired friend, the trout, is looking for meat—same as some fellow fishermen. I've never yet met a fisherman the size of whose brain isn't greater than the total size of most the trout he has caught—which includes body, fins, and guts! Quality of brains may be open to debate, but the law of averages on size favors man.

Which brings me back to a certain day and certain fish on

the Schoharie Creek, in a lovely stretch of pocket water, near a really big pocket of deep, heavy water, I like to call "the icebox." I've fished this water many times, always carefully. On this trip it was a bit low, and some of the pockets could be evaluated just a little more clearly than normally. I noticed a rock, just a few inches above the water, which I'd never seen above water before. My cast was quickly made and not quite right. There was a quick rise and turn—a lightly pricked fish—and a slack line. It was a good Brownie of at least two pounds and I saw his yellow belly. He'd been around more than three weeks. Naturally I said something, very quietly. Also I examined the barb on my hook, and rested the fish.

Many more casts and no more rises. To the best of my ability, I had tried to imitate a hatch. There was no flash, let alone rise. Maybe his mouth was sore. What should I do? That was my problem. It was definite, there was nothing to do now—or was there? Damn it, I wanted that fish! A hasty and second class cast shouldn't deprive me of the best fish of the month.

Here I was, standing in exactly the same spot, and I had exactly the same head on the same shoulders. Should I use it? Good idea! I really studied that water and the bottom beneath it. I knew where the trout fed and at least one fly he liked. How should that fly be presented—and from where, and when?

Three or four hours later I came back and planned my approach as if I'd not eaten for a week and there were no other fish in the stream. I came up close to the left hand bank and did my honest best to make my two hundred-pounds-plus really dainty. The rock was toward mid-stream but I couldn't get below it because of the depth of heavy water. Out came a new tippet and a brand new fly of the same size and pattern that had participated in the morning's tragedy.

There were high alders beside me but I could cast directly upstream. The water had a fast glide of about three feet and then part of its one-foot width slipped around and partly under the rock which sheltered my playmate. There were intermittent gusts of wind. From my morning studies, I knew I must place my fly at the top of the run so it would go by the rock within an inch or two. My trout should really have a chance to sink his molars into this one, head on. There should be no quick foray into the current, no quick turn with a sore lip, and then back to the rock.

False casting, I was not quite sure of myself! Upstream another eight feet—more false casting and then a ten-minute wait to be sure his majesty had not been disturbed. This fish cost a whole pack of cigarettes. He rose to a natural. All was in order. My brains apparently were proven. Now it was a question of skill. My problem was to send the fly twenty-five or thirty feet upstream and have the leader curl to the right, depositing my fly on the far upper end, and the far side, of a one-by-three foot run—I hoped without drag.

More false casting, and when the breeze seemed right—the world hung in the balance. A really perfect cast, a perfect float, a perfect strike, and I was fast to my fish! Now my skill was being tested. Would it or I be found wanting?

A run upstream. Keep the line tight but not too tight. He's heading down—get that line in! A head shaking contest—don't let him wear a hole in his lip. Over the rock—Oh, my Lord—O.K.—tight lines again, less chance for a casualty here. Every bit of concentration I have is on that fish! Could it be that he is tiring? Yes—but Bigelow be careful! Don't lose him! You're all right so far—but—yes, you're O.K. so far! This is a good fish—better than you thought. He's heading for the glory trail!

Here was triumph—my big brain had worked for several hours. Here was my victory—my skill had been used in its entirety. Here was satisfaction, even in the anticipation of telling the story that evening, and for years to come. Future generations should hear about the "icebox trout" which was growing steadily weaker. I stood in six inches of water and brought that old spotted yellow belly in above me, on his side.

Everything's under control! I edged over to the bank and tried to lift that fish ashore by the leader. Of course if fell off! Of course I made a grab! Of course I missed! Of course I ended on hands and knees! Of course I didn't swear! I just stayed on my knees!

There are various morals to this story which any reader with a mediocre brain can supply. Any fisherman of modest skill can tell me some things I might have done. Neither can tell me I'm dishonest. A lesser man might write how he triumphantly released the hook, carefully held the trout 'til he recovered, and sped away flipping his tail in gratitude for the magnamity of supreme skill and brains!

What really tees me off is how in the name of fifty years fishing could a man be such a consumate jackass? Please don't tell me!

The Bigelow Pool

SOME PEOPLE GAIN AWARDS, certificates, and medals for achievement in their chosen field, or for meritorious service in the public interest. Sometimes they are remembered in later years with statues and monuments. Think of what the cherry tree did for George Washington's memory! I have no record of his ever having been a trout fisherman.

Other persons, who either do or do not deserve the same degree of public or private acclaim, may actually seek such things. Breathes there a newspaper editor who has not been beseached for a supporting editorial or slanted news—particularly one praising Joe Zilch for his "peerless leadership and never ending labors in the cause of . . ." Joe Zilch?

The title of this story tends to make me believe the real heros are those who through their own stupidity and probably because they opened their mouths too wide, backed into their reward unknowingly. The safeguard against vanity in such situations is that, in many cases, only a very limited number of people ever know about such an award, as a trout pool bearing an unknown fisherman's name. It does not appear in Conservation Department annals, roadmaps or learned papers on particular streams or rivers.

It happened to me because I couldn't keep my big mouth shut. Heaven forbid that you think because a maximum of twenty-five people knew about it that I now publicize the tiosy. I didn't even name the pool! Probably at least twenty of the men who knew have forgotten. If those men have the dough and brains to buy this book, I am certain the recollection will give a chuckle and I'll be partially reimbursed for the treatment they gave and may give me again. The real purpose of this story is to recall some wonderful times and to illustrate that when your neck gets extended, you can back into what you least expected!

For about twenty-five years, that I have lived and loved, a lot of good fellows, who were excellent to "less so" fishermen, went to the Westkill Tavern Club in Westkill, Green County, near the Schoharie Creek. It has since burned down, so the camaraderie of the years can never be the same here again. However, the stream itself had other advantages to me over other Catskill streams. There were fewer people on it watching trout or a weekend fisherman from Greenwich. There were all kinds of water and even on crowded weekends, if you knew your stuff, you could generally be alone. The fish were there and you could find places to search for them. You did not have to follow the hatchery truck. The Beaverkill, the Esopus, the Willowemoc, the East Branch of the Delaware, and their feeder streams all have their virtues—but I liked the combination of everything best at Westkill.

In 1946, after an exhausting effort, I finally convinced myself I should spend the month of May on the Schoharie. I made side trips and, to be truthful, sometimes caught more fish. It is also true that 1946 was a banner year. I really learned something about the water and in the intervening years have relied on that experience. It is also true that the fish I kept that year averaged thirteen inches. That was pretty good for then, and, I would add, now.

At that time, the group of characters was in its glory. Some have gone to their reward. Some have had to quit fishing or have retired to distant parts. Art Flick has retired from every-

thing but fishing and wisecracking. His *Streamside Guide* has become a collector's item. A steadily dwindling number of oldtimers go back, I am certain, to seek just as hard-to-kindle old memories as to capture educated trout. They hope to see old friends never seen anywhere else.

These things are cherished. They are as much a part of living as the trout. There's a classification of each man's abilities: how far you can go, other talents, stories told and retold, even a "pecking order." For instance, there were two inseparables. Both were top notch fishermen. They lived at least five hundred miles apart. They were known as "Worse" and "Worser." "Worser" was accused of more persistence than "Worse"!

Well, to get back to the Bigelow Pool and the year 1946, way downstream the Bataviakill flows into the Schoharie. Facing downstream, the Bataviakill comes in from the right over a good riffle and the Schoharie comes down and then riffles against the far bank. After joining with two frequently different colored waters, the Batavia muddy and the Schoharie clear, it becomes a deep and fairly steady and powerful run before flattening out into a long wide pool.

I've never gone all the way down the pool to fish up, except a few times under discouraging conditions. From experience, or if you choose, habit, I nearly always fished three or four hundred feet only, always the same way—dry. My car would be left in the meadow. I'd cross the Bataviakill and walk down on the stones or high water beach to between the third and fourth big rocks downstream, put on my Gray Fox Variant and, depending on water height, work into the side current from knees to waist height. Then there'd be a wait to rest the water a bit and see if any fish were rising and where. I liked the late afternoon and early evening best. The fishing I did slowly, and really covered all the water ahead and across, as I cautiously inched myself upstream, usually with stops and rests not over every six feet. When the water was up, it took a long and careful cast to reach across to the far side water. There was usually a strike and, in these years, a number of small ones tossed back. As I neared the second rock, the care increased. If the trout were working, there were interesting currents around these two rocks, and all the way up to the first rock there were spots across the stream that could not be overlooked. The fishing was intriguing enough to prevent boredom and the reward of a few keepers could be satisfying. Thoughtful and careful fishing was not mentally or physically exhausting, but enough to keep one alive mentally. Besides, you never knew what animals you'd see on the far bank, or hear on the hill above. The complete freedom from conscious thinking of anything else was deeply satisfying to me. It still is, though the fish aren't as numerous as in a few banner years.

The particular day of which I write, was the very last one of my month of May holiday. I'd gone through my routine, kept a couple of decent fish, put back several small ones and taken far and away more time to complete this trip than usual. It was my last chance. It was time for the second phase, as the sun was down and dusk was in the offing. At this time, in order not to waste precious water and try other methods, I'd switch to a Bucktail, nearly always a Black Nosed Dace, and fish back down the water I'd just covered with a dry fly. Here, the first rock many times harbored a good trout. This evening there was nothing there, and the dusk was on its way. I've never learned to fish a dry after dark. I can't see to change it, or if the barb is gone. Maybe it's just experience with frustration of every kind.

The second rocks—I'll reach them shortly—maybe I can do so now. A long line doesn't have the dangers with a Bucktail it does with a dry. A couple more steps and another cast. Holy sufferin' catfish! As I lifted my Bucktail for the next cast, the biggest trout I'd ever seen stream fishing came out of water in a big, beautifully arching jump right after my Bucktail! Did I prick him? I don't know. Maybe he touched or didn't, but my reflex cast was back in his water immediately! I didn't have time to do anything but see his arching beauty and he was gone—all except the picture. That picture is still with me.

It was my last day. I just had to leave after breakfast. Naturally I stayed on, and on, and on and fished that fifty feet over, and over, and over. There was no action. In due course I stumbled back across the Bataviakill, took off my waders under the car headlights, and drove slowly and morosely back to the lighted bar of the Westkill Tavern Club. I was the last man in and I'm usually among the first. There's no doubt by this time that I was more than morose. Maybe the word is either disgusted or mad. The reaction had grown stronger as I drove. The fishing was all over. This had to happen to me—and I just couldn't stay longer! My holiday was already the longest of a lifetime. Twenty years later the blood pressure still rises—the last day!

At any rate, as I came through the door, eight or ten of these oldtimers looked around, and then the words came.

"What happened to you, we were getting worried!"

"Any luck—you're out so late!"

"Look at this!"

The crowd parted and there on the bar was a three pound Brownie. What ever got into me I don't know, but out of my mouth came the words, "Where I came from, we use those for bait!" Now it was their turn! I took quite a shellacking, which was justified. I also paced the floor. The needles were brushed off in thickets. Two drinks, I'm informed, were accepted with no word of thanks, just a few more expletives about sugar plums and Sound Old Bankers. Twice, I am told, I walked into the wall. Flick claimed I loosened a pillar. Someone added it was my language not my body that did it. Phooey on that stuff! My fish was still there and I had to leave after breakfast!

Finally both legs and tongue gave out. I was assisted to a chair. They wanted something besides entertainment. Two more drinks were forced on me. This wasn't a matter of generosity but was done on purpose! The questions started. All were from interested persons. Some were designed to be descreet, some were blunt and some were furtive and evil! All were designed to enable someone else to catch my fish! I could see him being ignominiously trampled to death by a group of irreverent stinkers!

So the answer to this story is that sometimes you earn awards, sometimes you acquire distinction, sometimes you create something of merit for which you receive credit. Sometimes also, you back into having a pool named after you. I must say that the Bigelow seemed to gain standing over the next couple of weeks as both Art Flick and another top notch fisherman hooked into presumably the same fish. Neither landed him. One broke a leader.

Much later on, one man said seven or eight pounds and the other one over five. I didn't want to again stick my neck out by saying anything! Besides, I'd backed into "The Bigelow Pool" and had to preserve something!

Fishing with the Distaff

SOMETIMES TWO FISHERMEN fish together year after year. Sometimes they are "overly enthusiastic," hard working and, publicly at least, "purists." Once in a long while, over the years I knew them, these two brought their wives. Only once do I recall that the wives fished. I haven't seen them in recent years. That is probably my misfortune, but this is life on our piscatorial pathway. We come and we go. We take up fishing; we continue it and somctimes we give it up. This is regrettable, but even fishermen must face life.

These "saintly souls" always came together, went together and fished together. They started in the early morning, whether it was hot or cold or wet or dry. I always think of them and a little verse I saw in the London Underground forty years ago. Their fishing fitted the verse:

Whether the weather be cold,
Whether the weather be hot,
Whether the weather be dry
Of whether the weather be not,
We must weather the weather
Whatever the weather,
Whether we like it or not.

The necessity of food and drink at eventide generally brought them in, but not if the fishing was good. Furthermore, they had two nice wives.

One morning the tour of duty was held up almost ten minutes because these charming ladies expressed a determination to fish. Although their feet were firmly planted and their gaze at their respective husbands was strictly eyeball to eyeball, the gentlemen appeared impatient even under such terrifying circumstances. Finally one of them conceded defeat, dug into the debris in the trunk of the car and handed out two rusty telescopic steel poles. Look up "distaff" in your dictionary—it fits the case in a couple of ways. It seemed unusual that any deeply dedicated fisherman should have such stuff in his car. However I had learned enough not to butt in on a family situation, so I merely observed the delivery and listened to the comment.

"Here are some hooks. Get Joe to get you some worms. We're late!"

The hooks must have been for either codfish or jigging suckers. As this distinctly was not my business, I gradually moved off into the heat of the day.

My own day was hot and seemed long as well as unsuccessful. Those inexperienced but very determined females prayed on my mind all day as I also struggled with the fish, the heat and myself. It seemed, shall we say, unfortunate on a day like this that two charming innocents should be equipped with rusted astronomic elongations of metal and miniature gaffs. They deserved the finest Tonkin Cane.

Finally I gave up, came in, peeled off the waders and sought a rocking chair and peace on the porch. There were the wives. I have seen women when they were cool as cucumbers. We have heard of the cat that swallowed the canary. Here was a couple of cuties who had both swallowed the canary and were cool as cucumbers. Something, but something, was up. Bigelow, this may be interesting. You don't know what's up, but the air has a distinct aroma. Something is going to happen and you want to be there.

Supper was served at six so that those who wished to get the evening fishing could rush out with appropriate indigestion. At precisely eleven minutes before this hour, the boys, who had run off so impatiently in the morning, drifted in slowly. The wheels on their car seemed to wobble. They left it in the middle of the parking lot. One got out each side. Both were sunburned, sweaty and appeared exhausted. There were no cheery waves to their wives. With glassy eyes they crawled into the bar.

"Two Tom Collins."

There was brief silence punctuated only by two gulps per glass.

"Two more Collins."

Out of the corner of my eye I could see them down half each glass, pick up the misty remainder and head slowly toward us on the porch. They slumped into adjoining chairs. One good wife opened the conversation.

"Did you have a good day?"

"No."

"Did you catch any fish?"

"No."

"Was it warm?"

"Hotter than hell!"

"That's funny, it wasn't bad here. Do you want some sunburn lotion?"

"Not now."

"Like another Collins, I'll get it for you."

"Good idea!"

The drinks arrived in due course and as the two started to soak them up, old man Bigelow had to stick his nose into the situation. This was stupid. To say my life was in danger would be absurd; they didn't have that much strength. However, sentiment was mauled and a beautiful friendship might have been endangered when I said, "Your wives have been fishing too."

"Yeah?"

After a long silence during which the rest of us said nothing, and they looked into their third Collins, one of the cuties added, "We enjoyed it."

"Good, let's eat."

"Finish your drink."

Finally one of them saw the light.

"Did you gals fish all day in this heat?"

"Only this morning, we got tired."

"So did we."

"Where do you think we fished?"

"I haven't the slightest idea. Where?"

"Near here."

"Where near here?"

"In the culvert across the road."

Three Collins brought their normal laughter.

"Did you catch anything?"

"A couple."

"What were they?"

"Maybe you can tell us. Would you like to see them?"

"Oh I guess so."

"They are on ice at the bar."

This I had to see. The men knew the location as they knew the stream. The girls trailed them with an exchange of female radar signals and canary smiles. The air was shattered by all sorts of things, cuss words, comments, positive expressions of disbelief and downright accusations! There were two nice trout!

During supper I sat at another table. My own nose was in the soup. Two other male noses followed suit. The gals dined on vitamin fed canaries and warmed over cucumbers. Fishing conversation was not on the menu.

Artistic Dunking

"PRIDE GOETH BEFORE A FALL." It is my observation that any enthusiastic trout fisherman has many times and for many reasons found his head where his heels ought to be in the cold, cold water. It seems part of the scheme of things that this is so, whether we like it or not. It is also my observation that it happens more to the young than to the old. The young fellows seem, in their blithe enthusiasms and confidence in their strength, to be consistently able to get wet in their endeavor to fulfill the ambition of the moment. The old geezers have been there before. They are cautious about their balance. With age comes conservatism. Other things are true also. As Rabelais pointed out so aptly, the human race does fundamentally enjoy somebody else's pratfall. In this respect at least, the old resemble the young and the young resemble the old, and Rabelais had the number of both.

My point in this story is that the dunkings should at least be artistic. With age comes pride and therefore I remember only three of the immersions which I suffered. Regardless of what you think, in my opinion they were artistic.

The first happened many years ago in the days of my youth when I was utterly convinced that hobs were the only safe means of keeping reasonably upright. I now have both hobs and felts because streams are different. I have less confidence in my feet and perhaps more in my head. Fundamentally even fishermen should rely most on their heads!

On the East Branch of the Delaware there is a long slate slab, maybe thirty feet, which the water comes over from end to end with the depth depending on the level of the water. In prior years I had fished it several times and it shot off into white water and a short deep pool. I used worms much more frequently those days because I went out nearly every April 1st.

This particular morning I was in a rush to get out early. There was still a trace of ice at the streamside and the water was high. With bait, the proper approach was to get on the slate and float the line and the worm down deep into the pool. This I did perfectly. The water was high; the morning was early. It was April and the temperature was low! I got my worm into absolutely perfect position and was standing comfortably with the fast water up to about the calf of my leg. It was time for a cigarette. Whether it was the shift in the weight of the package or fate just took a hand, I never knew. My feet started to move in complete unison. I had never faced this situation before. Inch by inch we gained momentum. Inch by inch we approached the inevitable. In due course, without my moving a foot, fate and I met eyeball to eyeball!

I never did hit bottom. I came up the other end of the pool. I still had my rod! My equanimity was lacking! Scrambling out shivering madly (no false teeth then) I could barely move with waders full of ice water. There was only one thing to do and that was park my fanny on the ground with my elbows and lift my tootsies as high in the air as I could. In my weakened condition, the second flood was colder than the first! There was no question on what the next step should be. I ran a half mile, waders and all, and at seven o'clock in the morning resorted to bourbon!

This I thought was fairly good for a beginner and for some years I had only the wettings normal to my age. But after say

ARTISTIC DUNKING

ten years, I fished the Housatonic in Connecticut in the neighborhood of Cornwall Bridge. The Housatonic water level is subject to the control of the power company and anybody who gets out reasonably deep had better plan his return to shore in advance.

I had had two days, one a complete bust, but the second day I had gotten way out and caught half a dozen fish in the heat of the day, on a hair fly and a very long sinking line. The afternoon and evening produced no results. On the third day, the obvious was to try the hair fly and the long line again. Once more I worked my way out to the same spot and was within two inches of the top of my waders, standing on a stone. The water looked as if it was rising. There were no dice or explanations. I knew my way back. I went with care and caution and arrived within ten feet of the shore in a current a couple of feet deep and fast. The root of all evil caught my foot, I twisted and went down. The current came in the back of my waders. This, ladies and gentlemen, is what is called "bumping the bottom." It is a turn of phraseology I have learned to appreciate. For forty feet I bumped the bottom and the bottom bumped me! I felt as if the whole damned river was in my back and that I had outboard motors on both feet. I couldn't stop! Next time you want to take a spill, try doing a couple of dozen bumps in thirty seconds! It's exhilarating! I am in favor of rubber stones in all fast trout water.

You would think that the old folks would really learn something by experience, but they don't always. A couple of years ago I was fishing some good fast pocket water on the Schoharie Creek and I had, as a matter of fact, caught a couple of decent fish and saw a good one rising in a small pool ahead. There was only one way to get there and that was to clamber along the side of the bank. This was pretty well covered with the driftwood and rubbish remaining from the spring high water. I kept my eyes on the fish rising. This was a mistake. One should sometimes watch one's feet. One of mine went through. Fortunately I was able to turn as I fell, so my knee joint permitted me to fall without breaking my leg! Skill, my friends, skill plus a lot of that stuff called luck that we need to fish with.

I came down all right, the only thing was that my whole body lay at a forty-five degree angle down from my knee with my head touching the water! There I was! Nothing broken! Head in the soup; knees in the air and one foot God knows where. The question was what to do about it. I couldn't move the foot to right or left or forward. I was holding my rod from force of habit and I couldn't get myself up! My head moved around and saw that behind me was some nice deep, clear water. There was only one thing to do. I had time to reconcile myself to my fate. The opportunity for anticipation was perfect. Any alternative was nil. My resolve was made.

Slowly and carefully I lifted the knee straight up. The foot came clear. The head, the neck, the shoulders and finally my tummy followed by legs slid as gracefully as a porpoise into the pool. It was a back dive in slow motion. This I count as my greatest artistic achievement in dunking! I came up refreshed and with satisfaction pulled off most of my clothes for a sun drying operation.

As I dryed I laughed at myself. Is there any better medicine? Who on earth, with all the possibilities that trout fishing holds, would want to sit in an anchored boat and fish with bait?

THE EAST

The East, or the Learning Process

MY GRANDSONS started the learning process in regard to fish at approximately five years of age. I know I am learning still, at least in regard to fish. There is always an overlap in the acquisition of knowledge or experience and neither I nor anyone else can do all their trout homework in the Catskills, the East, the West or Abroad, which are arbitrary but convenient divisions of this book. For that matter, our lessons are not assigned on a per annum basis, nor does each fisherman learn the same thing at the same time.

However, after a beginning and the usual tendencies to be dogmatic, one does see "greener fields" in other areas than one's own back yard. You hear about the fishing somewhere else. You would like to try it sometime. The student or the realist comes to realize that the hard boiled egg (or dogma) may not always taste as well as one scrambled—soft. The income may permit more travel. Enthusiasms become more tempered and thoughtful. You even begin to think more of the things you don't know or can't understand. This may be the approach to greatness, if you are so inclined, but for ordinary mortals it is the turning point to reasonable competence.

I am still using up slowly some flies bought almost forty years ago. Some are beauts. Today I don't use over half a dozen flies regularly. Once in a long while and after real vicissitude, I still use a fan wing Royal Coachman on a No. 8 hook. I was told about it. It works. Why I don't know.

A friend and I were fishing Dry Brook. We both were fishing Brown Bivisibles. He had a twelve hook and was catching none. I had a fourteen and was doing fine. We switched flies. He got fish and I didn't. Don't tell me the average trout has a micrometer, but he may at that.

In Kamloops, my son-in-law and I were getting skunked. That night he tied three inches of black marabou on a short shank hook. The next day we got trout on these leeches and for Christmas I had to buy up all the black marabou in New York City!

Looking at the water from a bridge, I have several times taken a bit of cellophane from my cigarettes, twisted it and let it flutter to the water. This has brought a rise often enough for me to give it limited testing.

Wet flies are normally fished downstream. One day I was getting nothing until a friend, who was loaded, pointed out that if I stayed on my knees and fished upstream I would do better. I did. The trout all had Polaroid glasses!

One hot day, three of us met for lunch on a high bank overlooking a pool about 250 feet long. We had had a hard morning. A mild hatch started and there seemed to be four fish for every fly. We spread ourselves out in the pool and in the next hour and a half we each hooked, landed and returned at least forty fish!

A similar thing happened in Pine Creek, Pennsylvania. We found the fish very shy and the snakes troublesome during the day. That evening those very shy fish were bumping our waders and not taking our flies. Why, oh why? Please tell me.

With all our fancy gear, sophistication and perhaps knowledge, it was interesting to note that in Chile many Indians wrapped a line around a tin can. They put a spoon on the end of the line and a stick loosely through both ends of the can.

THE FISH WERE VERY SHY... ABOUT FLIES!

The spoon was swung around the head, the can rattled like a jet and the Indians caught their trout.

Maybe these things are why we keep at it. It gives us a chance to develop our individual theories so that momentarily we can hope to plant our footsies on the ladder of greatness.

Four of a Kind

IN JUNE 1934 the bank holiday was behind us, but problems weren't. Everybody had 'em—including banks. Our Executive Committee met at four one Tuesday and examined my agenda. Following this effort, someone said, "Bigelow, these are the same problems we had last week. You're the President now, you solve 'em!" The meeting adjourned at four-thirty P.M. eastern daylight saving time.

These captains and kings didn't know the answers. They also knew that I didn't either. All have long since departed. They can't deny the story now. I don't think they would anyway, for both fishing and banking problems were solved.

Bigelow had just been made President. The weight of the centuries was on his shoulders. He lived two blocks away with two children, one wife, one car, one rod and one pair of leaky boots—so he went fishing. Getting there was a long, hard drive of three and one-half miles from the Boston Post Road in the center of Greenwich, Connecticut.

Over the stream on a bridge with no sides and a short jounce across a Connecticut rotten granite dirt pathway. I parked by the only fifteen-foot pool in the entire trickle of water. The stream is now overwhelmed by ranch houses and our Water Company has a fine filtration plant—elsewhere.

Nothing rose in the pool so I started upstream casting a short line, of necessity with care, and from force of habit getting the normal number of mishaps. My business puzzlement was such that even my feet moved slowly. I stumbled less. This is important both in banking and fishing.

How could I keep the Sheriff off Tom's back?

Is it possible for me to cast left around that bush?

The Sheriff has to do his job too.

The cast wouldn't work for me. One step forward—slowly.

Tom's problems are slow motion also. Some of his customers will pay him someday.

Is that spot really the one I want to reach after all? There seems to be a pocket of deeper water still further to the left.

Tom's in deep water too!

Can I reach it if I lean over and just dap the fly? I think so, if I can just brace myself.

How many people owe Tom money—in big amounts? Are they decent? Are they willing to help?

If I stoop and lean over slowly, I can get my left hand on that rock. This is it! Can I hold it 'til I get that fly out? I can! I do! I dap! He has it! Make no mistake—he has it! No use bracing with the left hand. On my knees in the water. No room for maneuvers here! Come to papa, 'Thomas'! Horsing it is, but I can't help it! Well, I'll be damned! This fish has never heard of a hatchery in any of his twelve speckled inches! Those red and white fins of Mr. Thomas Salvelinus were exactly as Mother Nature intended they should be! Can't even lift him to the bank. The net's caught in the bushes of bankruptcy. Maybe I can hold rod and leader with my right hand. I can. I do. Poor devil, my big left hand has him just as hard as he has the fly.

He's really gorgeous! I've been talking to Thomas Salvelinus.

Tom's not as beautiful but they both have a clean, lean look. This has been careful stuff. Tom's entitled to that too. You know, I've been more patient than usual. Maybe the hard way is necessary at times. After all, it's the end result that counts.

That's Tom's problem too—mine also I might add. It doesn't make sense to write his loan off. He's not hopeless.

Hello, there's a small pool under the bank. Again! Less then five minutes and Salvelinus' first cousin lies beside him. This was no trick stuff—even the net worked. Maybe a bit more mental sweat is in order.

Perhaps a few phone calls this evening to see just what gives with Tom's other creditors.

Time for a cigarette. Two trout in this water in less then twenty minutes—twelve inch brookies.

Maybe the world will survive the depression.

Maybe, if I'm lucky, I'll get my limit? No I'm afraid not.

Has Tom reached his limit? I don't think so.

This isn't luck—this is hard work and fine!

He hasn't quit yet. Why should I?

Here we go again. Here's another good looking spot. No room for a back cast. Caution all over again. I've got to get close enough to control my back cast straight up.

Tom's been straight up, too.

No result in the foot of pocket. We'll try the side where the water comes round the rock.

It's just like going round Tom to some of his creditors.

Here we go again! Every one right out of the same mold! These fellows were born here and have grown up strong and free.

So's Tom. He's caught or out looking for food too. Maybe there is a solution. After all, I'm supposed to be President. If I can get some agreement with a few big creditors—maybe a little more time and money. Maybe there's no use. Maybe there's no thanks. What of it? I know if he has to start all over he'll pay me some day under any circumstances.

If I can get just one more trout I'll have one for each member of the family.

If I can get a rise from four creditors, I think Tom's problem may be solved, as well as the creditors', and mine.

In something short of a quarter mile, my disposition had vastly improved. The trees had become impossible. The watch said six o'clock eastern daylight saving time. Four fair-sized Brook Trout were taken from the creel, cleaned and carried home to the family. The kids found their old man as pleasant as he found them.

For about twenty years I tried to find out whether this could happen here again. It never did. I doubt if I caught two legal fish here in all those years! Tom paid. Dreams should be cherished. When we tamper, we cut ourselves down to size.

The Boy Next Door

I CAN POINT WITH PRIDE to starting this kid of eleven or twelve not only on a life of near crime and piscatorial murder, but with a flexible, artistic and determined outlook on life. He is now a first class fisherman; he is also a teacher. He could probably teach fishing better than those things he has to answer for, such as history, English, ultra-stupid Latin, or what have you.

Boys this age have insatiable curiosity. This is wonderful. They want to know the why and how of everything and apparently will find a way somehow to find out. They don't always remain silent in the acquisition of knowledge. I had been observed coming in and out of my home, in and out of waders, sometimes wearing my vest, sometimes with the rod strung up.

"Why did the waders go so high? Did I always go in that deep? What were the funny shoes for? Wouldn't he have to grow taller or could he get smaller waders? What was in the vest? What kind of a fly was this? What did I mean by a dry fly? What is a tapered line? What was the right length of leader? Could he hold the rod?"

There's only one thing to do and that is submit gracefully. If you don't, the questions continue. So I did. I finally got out an inexpensive rod, a line that was almost ready for the discard, an old leader and a small piece of old handkerchief. We set a child's hoop on the front lawn and we started practicing.

If his pupils study their history as well as he studied casting, the less intriguing periods of history will not be forgotten by the next generation. In between his casts was a question, or two, or three, or more, but it was also flattering to see that he listened to what I said—even if I yelled at him. I can yell pretty well and he could listen even better.

It wasn't long before his rod was stopping at twelve o'clock, before he was waiting for the pull of the back cast and before his line was dropping as it should with the little tag of handkerchief in the center of the hoop.

The inevitable question came, as I knew it must. "Mr. B, will you take me fishing?" By this time I was hooked, so we made a date. Laziness or selfishness didn't persuade me to take him to a good stream as I should have, so I took him to a poor one nearby. As we walked along the stream towards a particular spot, I pointed out a few things and let him cast over live water.

When we got to the one particular spot where there might be a trout, we stopped and I explained very carefully just how I thought he should fish, where he should put the fly to get the best float and all over again how he should bring it up from the water. The kid was good. Again he followed instructions and praise be to all ye gods and little fishes, a trout rose and took!

Man oh man! Boy oh boy! Man and boy! Boy and man! Hell and high water! He landed the fish! I tied a bowknot in his grin at the back of his head. Naturally we had to try awhile more and naturally that was the only fish.

The following week he went away to a boy's camp for six weeks. I felt positively noble and he had had fun. I remembered, and promised myself to take him again. These ruminations always have an indefinite date and one day I came home late and there he was, sitting on the steps.

"Mr. B, Mr. B! I caught a big one way up in Maine. I caught it all by myself! Can you see it now?" The grin was still as big and when we got to his kitchen there was a four pound small mouth bass! It had been caught in Maine. It was cold. It had not been cleaned. It had not been scaled. It looked fresh. He wanted me to help him eat it. I like fresh fish. I didn't want to hurt the boy's feelings nor did I want any form of ptomaine poisioning.

"George, when did you catch the fish?"

"Last night."

"When did you get on the train?"

"Eight o'clock this morning."

"How did you carry the fish?"

"This way," and he held it up.

"But you were on the train." Never did I underestimate a boy's ingenuity so badly. "How did you keep it fresh?"

"Mr. B, when the conductor wasn't around I put it on the ice in the water cooler."

We both consumed the fish with gusto.

Naming a Fly

OLD FISHERMEN HAVE FRIENDS they enjoy watching. It's always because they are friends we wish well. Generally the feeling is enhanced because they do a beautiful job of casting and they seem to have the knowledge or instinct of where and how to catch fish. Once in awhile they also are short and stocky. Why I don't know, but several such friends all seemed very bold waders. I'm close to six feet, heavy, and once strong, but I was always more cautious than these guys. I have taken my share of spills—I can't recall they did.

The particular friend I write about also wore bifocles and tied his own beautiful flies. He had it, and, from my standpoint we never fished together enough. Our last trip is the subject of this story.

It was a meadow stream. These always seem to be a psychological hazard because the damn cows seem to like meadows. Here it wasn't so bad however, because the animals appeared to be in another pasture and the stream itself ran between deeply cut banks. It twisted and turned enormously, and the water seemed to alternate between shallow spots and deep pools. It was almost a question of look for a rise, fish a pool, make a turn and do it again. Much of the time our heads were below the meadow and the real problem seemed only to keep the back cast high enough to avoid the bank.

He went first. I followed by two or more hundred feet. If I

saw him, I had the pleasure of watching him handle his rod. I also knew I was getting too close and should wait. He was telling me when to rest the fish, and simultaneously giving me a lesson in how to catch them. When he disappeared I knew I could go ahead again.

Gradually the stream straightened a bit. He was about three hundred feet ahead and I could see him. He was casting a long line and doing it beautifully. He seemed to be fishing for a particular fish and doing it very carefully. He changed his fly and I watched. I also noted that even his long line never touched the bank as mine sometimes did. I was too far away to see his fly. As a matter of fact, I rarely got the glint of line, but it didn't catch and I could watch him strip it after each cast.

After watching a number of his casts with the new fly, I began looking over my own water when I heard his yell. He'd hooked something all right! Look at that rod bend! It's bending down stream! He's got to turn. He can't play this fish over his shoulder! Oh, Oh—he slips, he tries and can't catch himself. Down he goes, but he's good—and I mean good! His rod's held above him as he sits down. He grabs the reel and gets his knuckles busted! What gives? The rod's straight up! He starts scrambling up the bank. Me too, Bud, this I've got to see. He runs! I run!

What the hell? His glasses are gone and he drops his rod. He's running all scrunched over and every twenty feet or so he tries to grab something in the grass! I'm getting closer. He sits down again but this time he has hold of something. I'm close enough now to see his line and backing straighten out in mid-air, while he holds on for dear life. It's pointing away from the stream! He's swearing—just as beautifully as he fished. That is considerable praise.

The moral of this story is that the backing should be firmly fastened to the reel spool when fishing—with a cow's ear!

Piscatorial and Other Genealogy

EVER SINCE THE PILGRIMS LANDED, Salvelinus Fontinalis has been the trout pictured in American song and story. He has always been a delight to all boys and some men. Even today there are sentimental thousands. While not personally acquainted with Indian culture, I have no doubt whatsoever that the Indians must have felt much the same way and they too must have known good food when they saw it. When the Pilgrims had a slightly pinched tummy, can you imagine anything much better than first gazing on Fontinalis's georgeous colors and symmetry and then removing the pinch from the mid-section, all with due reverence?

Fontinalis also has other virtues including his willingness to cooperate with man. In fact, he has trusted man much too much! In consequence, he has been pushed around by the transplants and invaders of the last century, as well as suffering from pollution, shelter removed from his home and perhaps even chopped to small bits by energetic turbines of all kinds.

In my opinion, Fontinalis has not only been the most beautiful trout to behold and the best to eat, but the easiest to catch. Even the millions that our hatcheries spew forth to live briefly before the water gets too warm for them to survive, have inherited the instinct to cooperate with man. They have also been proven capable of seduction by practically all man's iniquitous lures. I think we will all admit he is a gracious friend to put up with all this deceit and probably has been since time immemorial, or certainly during recorded history, Indian, Pilgrim or Pilgrim's progeny.

Less sentimental people would say that a brook trout is dumb. Sometimes I've been suspicious that there are some forms of animal life that might be considered dumber. Some of my friends consciously or otherwise researched this idea and created a monument of their own to dear old Fontinalis. They erected it in due course in a spot where he would be properly reverenced. Others like myself have taken it to our hearts.

In case your eyes are like mine, the inscription at the base of this trophy reads as follows:

SALVELINUS FONTINALIS
Discovered on the Westkill Creek
Westkill, Green County, N. Y.
July 1, 1952
By
Dr. George H. Vaugilluwe
E. John Hodges, A.A.
Authenticated by:
Arthur B. Flick, L.O.W. and E.A.
Arthur Ritter, R.W.
Said to be the petrified remains of a Pliocene
ancestor of our present day brook trout

A fisherman could conceivably be deceived by this illustration. I would therefore explain that one of the discoverers making a perfect cast of a No. 28 dry fly, hooked a piece of driftwood. The fine texture of the wood does not appear in this picture. The natural shape is there but my friends being artists at heart, always sought improvement. This was done by delicately inserting a dorsal fin of similar wood, carefully cutting out an eye socket or two and further delineating the lines of the

PISCATORIAL & OTHER GENEALOGY

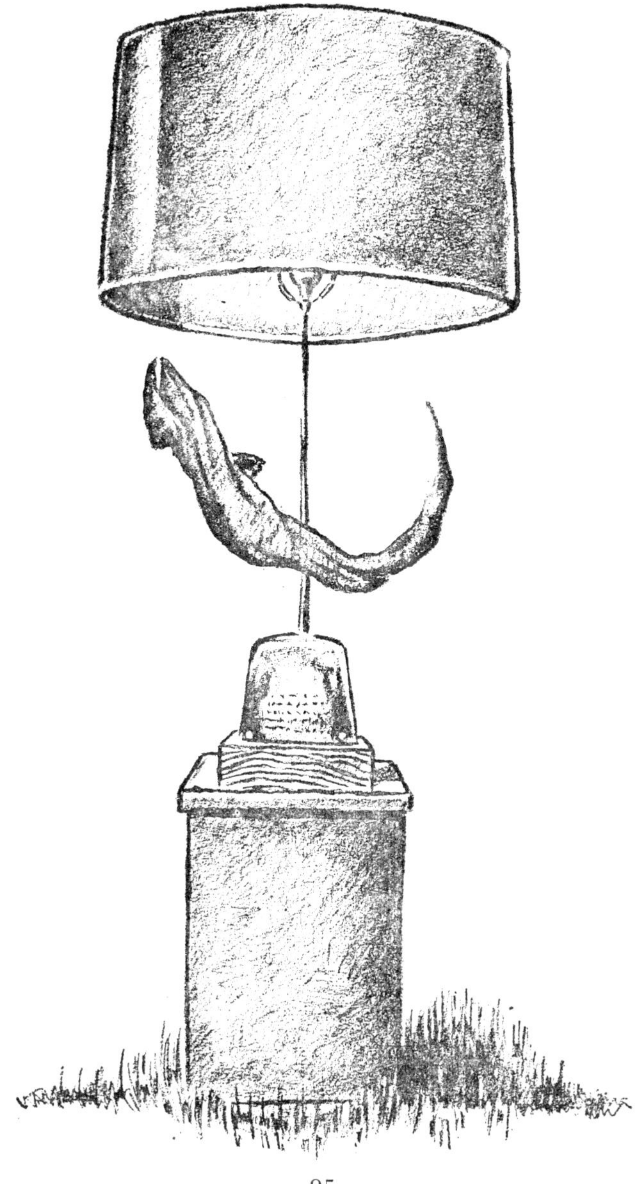

jaw. It is a throughly artistic job. It was not my good fortune to be present at the presentation ceremony, but I have no doubt whatever that suitable libations were poured, as they should have been. The Westkill Tavern at that time was in full swing and the whole creation was placed in a position of prominence in the lounge.

For years the fishermen of May and June invariably greeted this old friend. Unfortunately the Flicks have retired from the business and the Tavern has burned down. The story is prevalent that Mr. and Mrs. Flick when they retired insisted, in fact demanded, that this momento be taken with them and it now reposes in their living room where a few old friends like myself periodically make proper obeisance.

You will notice, dear reader, that I have carefully mentioned May and June. If you are familiar with the Catskills, you will realize that the fishing is apt to slow down in July and that the group of vacationers changes. However, our staunch friend, Salvelinus Fontinalis, Esquire, remained true to his principles and surveyed the lounge with a friendly eye from January through December. Visitors came and went. They couldn't fail to see this tribute to history. It dominated the room and it seemed to dominate the interest even of the non-fishermen.

There were all sorts of comments and questions, including, "What kind of a fish is that?" Some of the weightier thinkers would speculate on the dates connected with the Pliocene Era. These ran anywhere from 1926 to the Book of Genesis. There really was an element of confusion. The admiration was evident. The understanding was nil. Three thousand four hundred twenty-seven students of archeology were created on the spot. Such discussions immediately brought forth interpretations of the degrees accorded those sterling gentlemen mentioned in the plaque.

Mr. John Hodges, the fish creator, had his A.A. described as Andrew Ananious or Alcoholics Anonymous. John prescribed the A.A. as standing for "Amateur Angler." Actually he was a modest gentleman who understood humor. Like Rabelais, he realized we laugh at somebody else's pratfall. The prats were all over the place during July and August, particularly if there was a fisherman there to listen.

Practical jokers can be a pain in the neck or can furnish genuine amusement. This one furnished quiet amusement to the fishermen at the expense of the non-fishermen. I have never heard of so many pratfalls created with such subtlety.

Obviously if you have borne with me so far, you may be curious as to what L.O.W. and E.A. following the name of Arthur B. Flick stand for. The answer is "Laird of Westkill" and "Expert Angler." Following Mr. Ritter, there appeared the letters "R.W." The two perpetrators of this creation again showed their impish approach. This stands for "Retired Wrestler." Mr. Ritter, long deceased, never was or could have been by any stretch of the imagination of his friends a retired wrestler!

As I have already said, the comments of July and August, when heard by true trout fishermen, were always listened to with wonder, and quiet pride in their own avocation. More insults were unconsciously handed to the elite than would otherwise have been possible. The elite were in this way reassured they were the elite! It is one reason I call my rod a rod and not a pole. It is one reason the blood pressure rises when someone says, "He's a trout fisherman" and some gook, to make conversation, starts talking about fishing for eels, codfish or carp. Those fish have culinary virtues, but they are not trout!

Salvelinus may be gradually departing his pristine glory. How much of the human race should he take with him?

The Three Graces

SOME OF YOU WISE GUYS will think of brunette, blonde and redhead. Look it up if you really find it necessary. The ancient Greeks had the gals all named and assigned each a characteristic. That's all right with me, but assuming you are lazy, I am combining the Greek and the Bigelow versions. You can take your choice as follows:

Ancient Greek Word	*Ancient Greek Characteristic*	*Bigelow (Getting Ancient)*
Euphrosne	Joyfulness	Brookie
Aglaia	Brightness	Rainbow
Thalia	Bloom	Brownie

All three were reported to be the daughters of Zeus and great pals of The Muses.

I love 'em all. The size and shape were generally the same and the length nearly always ten to eleven inches. Thalia was by far the most prolific or promiscuous locally.

Some years ago, we spent the month of July in Whitefield, New Hampshire, the home of my Three Graces. My wife doesn't fish. She stayed at the inn. The Three Graces—particularly Thalia—and Bigelow roamed about more. Bigelow found the Ammonoosuc River. An Indian encyclopedia is not readily available, but a literal translation might be "Home of

Euphrosne, Aglaia and Thalia." It's a delightful stream characterized by bloom, brightness and joyfulness. It had to be fished! From this background picture, problems and puzzlement stem.

The inn was just as delightful as the stream. It was largely inhabited by The Graces and their boyfriends of yesteryear—just like ourselves. Living was properly geared to the inhabitants. There were few problems besides Bigelow's. The meals were at appointed hours. They were delicious. I was chronically hungry—and nearly always overate. This meant a delightful nap in the early afternoon. Both my wife and I enjoy Bridge, provided there is early bed. This means an early start to prevent overbidding on the last rubber. No one overexerted. Very few others fished. Practically everyone liked to eat trout.

It all boiled down in the end to what might be called circumscribed fishing. I had to savor all the meals. My nap and the Bridge could not be overlooked. There always seemed to be someone who wanted to eat trout again—"They're so different from codfish." Here was a challenge I had to rise to and both the Ammonoosuc and I did fairly well in the two hours allotted each morning, and the afternoon, provided the last rubber didn't necessitate a long nap. All but once the hourly stipulations of the regime were conformed to. I provided fish. The pressure was enormous!

The first job was to look over the river, to drive up and down, and walk through some bushes. Of course I found some idyllic spots which numerous other people also considered idyllic. In fact, some looked so damn idyllic I felt sure the trout's preferences were the same as my own. We both stayed away! I also marked down some interesting stretches of pocket water, and a big pool below a dam of some sort which seemed suitable for evening fishing. Evenings had their problems and I never did get to it. Based on what I've heard, I hope to go back someday, or rather evening. On this trip other matters sidetracked the idea. I did however try a series of stretches with fair success, not enough to prevent trying other locations, but enough to justify continuing fishing. Not much is necessary.

During this process I found one nice swinging pool. Here, without moving over twenty feet, you could float your fly in big arcs and thoroughly cover the whole pool. Naturally I started at the bottom and fished up. There was no luck at first, although that water just had to have trout! They weren't for me.

Finally I got to the head of the pool and there was a vest pocket-sized junior deal before the water spread out to the big swing. A few careful casts and I hooked and landed a typical ten or eleven inch fish. He did not have as much perspicacity as his parsimonious relatives in the papa-sized pool below. The pool was rested and I fished through again, carefully and slowly. There was no action, so I went on upstream.

After several hundred feet, I came on a tiny pool or large pocket—take your choice. The second cast brought the brother of the first from the pool below. My allotted time span was short. The water above seemed more of a struggle than arrival at supper permitted. Back I went. The swinger had had a real rest. There were still a few minutes left so I wandered downstream a bit. There was a fast run, and part way across the bottom had fallen a tree trunk. This should be explored later.

The next day I did go back, went downstream, crossed the stream well above the tree trunk and got into position so I could fish the run and the tree trunk carefully from the far side. Virtue has its own reward, about eleven inches long. I fished on up and through the big swinger. My second fish was landed in exactly the same place on exactly the same fly as the preceding day. I decided to give the pool a real rest and fished on up to the big pocket when I landed number three in exactly the same spot as the day before!

There was time, so I went all the way back to my tree trunk

and fished all the way through again. There were absolutely no results—none. Driving back to dinner, I pondered the fact that two fish were taken at identical spots on two successive days. All were approximately the same size. To round things out, I revoked twice at the bridge table.

Day number three arrived in due course and back I went. Again three more fish from these identical spots. Again second time over and no sign of any fish. I hoped for four and finally got one quite a ways upstream. This was an expensive fish. The chef got a tip and mine host was placated with four trout. There were other troubles. I came in as other guests came out of the dining room. There was a positive chorus! "I've never fished but I do love to eat trout." "Hurry through your dinner, get indigestion." "Won't you play Bridge? Please don't revoke," and, "Get me some trout tomorrow." Ho hum and hearts and flowers!

The next day was monotonous. There were three fish the first time through and none the second. I used the same fly, caught practically identical fish and in definitely identical spots! You're beginning to get the idea. So was I. I never fished the same water over again a second time. I'd start below and fish once through and above. Sometimes I got four or five fish and, just once, six. However, never once in eleven days did I fail to get three trout, of the same size, in the identical spots.

These New Hampshire trout are not only perspicacious and parsimonious, but peripatetic as well. Papa was persistent, pleased and puzzled! He promised people promiscuously, and performed. How come?

Good Luck Only

HONESTY FORCES THE ADMISSION that Bigelow doesn't always get fish under the more adverse circumstances. This statement is made categorically. It's about time something was done to build up my integrity.

One August I was invited to spend a day at another fisherman's club. This was probably because with conditions at the time, the members had sense enough to stay away—not Bigelow! Half these members, incidently, had heart trouble. Even if my judgment was defective, I was more fortunate.

The clubhouse was near the end of a very small stream which was ten feet wide at the most, and came out of the hills above. The members had dredged out four or five large pools and cleaned out the brush around them to make casting simpler. They owned the headwaters and had wired the dam at the lower end of their property to prevent their numerous stocked fish from rushing madly downstream. If I were a fish, I am sure I would have tried either side of these pools to prevent being snagged or to escape the heat of the sun on unsheltered water.

I am not above catching fish under almost any circumstances, but this was not my preferred dish of tea. We had no comfort in it. My host was a good guy, a good fisherman, and had heart trouble. I did not remind him of his problem by saying, "Please could I fish upstream?" If you want the complete truth, I might add that it also occurred to me that rapidly running water upstream above man-made pools, plus natural shade, might be cooler and that the fish might have found that out also.

Up I went, wading the middle of the stream, six to ten feet wide and six to eighteen inches deep. The alders generally met overhead, but occasionally there was six inches of blue sky and hot sun. The water was clear and the gradient steep. The rocks were slippery and the day was really hot. There was no breeze amid the alders and the various insects had me down as the original Juicy Fruit.

It took me over twenty years to get away from a felt hat when fishing. This did the trick! It took another twenty to get a lighter and less sacred vest. I have got it. As it is implausible and as my honesty isn't impeccable, I would say it might take another twenty years to catch another easy fish.

Actually the fishing really was a struggle. First, you would sweat under any circumstances, and next, open spaces between the alders seemed to come only every few hundred feet. My shirt and handkerchief were just as wet as the stream. I would wipe off the sweat and wring out the handkerchief. Also, and as a practical matter, whenever I would come to an open pocket, I would have to stop to rest both myself and the water. There also had to be a smoke to help with the bugs.

Why do we do it? We like it! Smart? Oh boy!

After a really long struggle, I came to a place where there must have been at least fifty feet of open water. Right in front of me was a small pool and at the top of the open space was another. Both were up against the right hand bank. In between was a long and really fast run going under a cut bank. Directly in front of me, in the center of the stream was a dry gravel bar, which also ran about half way up the open space.

This was good water—the best I had seen, even with the alders directly behind my back. This should be handled with real care and the water should get a real rest. I fastened my fly in the holder. It was the old favorite, Grey Fox Variant, and I did have a nine foot leader. So I smoked quietly and let the sweat run off. My feet had been struggling and they got a rest here also. Even the faint breeze seemed to help blow the bugs downstream behind me. This also gave me a chance to hold my arms out and shift my vest a bit. This was really the best spot in my trek upstream, and it was time to carefully examine in detail the back cast problem. It was there all right. Another cigarette and an examination of the water ahead. Two feet forward to the base of the gravel bar to adjust the back cast to the water. Then more water study.

What's that! A flash in the riffle? It sure was! Again! That fish is working! I unhooked my fly and let the cigarette drop from my mouth. A false cast wasn't necessary. The rod and leader would do the trick. The fly lit about eighteen inches above the flash location, floated past the spot and I could see the rush of a fish downstream after it. He took! I lifted the rod tip. Between the rush of the fish, the rush of the water and my own strike, that fish ran right up on the gravel bar at my feet! I leaned down and picked him up! It was a nice pound and a half brown! This all happened in less time than it takes to tell. It all goes to show that while skill is desirable, it isn't always strictly necessary—or is it?

The Jumper Proves the Rule

PERIODICALLY A DEDICATED DRY FLY TROUT FISHERMAN can rationalize acceptance of landlocked salmon, Atlantic salmon or even Pacific salmon. Whether rationalized or not, he may even go beyond flies to bait. There's nothing wrong with these other fish or, for that matter, with the use of certain baits at certain times for certain fish. However, the procedure can make a habitual enthusiast furtive or something else. The state of mind is the real key. Maybe furtive is the wrong word. There's no doubt I'm nuts, but certainly bait seems less fastidious, even when more effective.

All this being partially true, it is gospel with some that a landlocked salmon is the jumpingest so and so that ever shook his head, fins, tail and gill covers above the water.

We were fishing the Big Eddy in the Penobscot River for these jumpers. The name of the pool is perfect. There's a dam with a lake above, white water below the dam, and also at the tail of a long long pool. True to habit, we'd been fishing everything we could reach wading, first with big dry flies and then bucktails and streamers. It was cold. So was the water. This had given periodic excuse to come ashore to change flies, warm up legs and torso and try from another position to reach new currents. Any success was composed exclusively of wind and weather, provided you like cold and rain! Sandwiches and hot coffee at noon was the first satisfaction of the day.

Our guide and boatman, however, was not satisfied with his stubborn and willful charges. In our weakened condition, the thought of wading back in, plus his pursuasive words, let him punish us into trying the canoe and a minnow.

Don't think our problems were over. It started to sleet. Slickers kept out most of the water. Glasses and guides could only be cleaned without any satisfaction or pleasure whatsoever. The bottom of a tin canoe has never yet been satisfactorily heated. The body problems were just reversed. Instead of cold feet and cool tail, it became cold tail and never mind the feet! You didn't have to use either in this situation, so on with the dance.

We followed instructions and we paddled up one side of the white water as far as we could go. The next step was a quick shift to fish down the other side of the white stuff. This brought enough interest from small fish to make me willing to let my body become steadily more cramped. The hands grew steadily colder from cleaning guides and glasses and from returning an occasional small fish. In due course, came the inevitable comment, "One more time around and I'll call it a day." Even the guide seemed depressed. By way of variety, the next comment was, "Let's reverse it, go up the far side and we can come down the near side and go home."

We did, and at the very peak of the guide's struggle with the current, I got a good solid strike. This fish was a good one and also well hooked. The line was kept tight. There was steady pressure. There were no great runs. I waited for the jumping in the best tradition of the species. There were none. I knew this fish was a good one. So did the guide. What kind of fish, anyway?

Oh no!!! This isn't right! This can't happen to me! No and no again! They're letting pulp logs through the spillway! The guide shuddered. I could feel it come from the other end of the canoe! It tingled my butt and stopped with my legs. He was smart, really smart. He guided that canoe backwards so I could handle the fish. He headed for quiet water, for the logs were something to be watched also. For awhile I could get the line above them, but they "pinged" that tin canoe ever more steadily.

We were both yelling. Those pine logs were really pungent—at least their description was. Now the guide was really backing that canoe downstream. No longer could I lift the line over the logs. It had to be under. Still the fish didn't jump! My rod tip was more below the water than above. I did keep the line tight. The "pings" were constant. The fish was either a gentleman or a jackass. It couldn't be a landlocked. He followed along with the "pings" until I heard the welcome scrunch of the canoe on the sand bar.

The guide yelled with emphasis, "Get out!" I replied with equal expletive, "I can't!" He made some damn fool comment and I told him to keep his mouth shut and help me out! He offered to take the rod. The blood went to my head! He grabbed an arm and I had to shake him off and switch the rod to the other hand. The tip remained below water. The line was tight. The fish did not run or jump! The logs kept coming! Great Day in the mornin', afternoon and evening!

Finally I go. it across to the poor abused guy that I couldn't stand up and that he just had to pick me up and out from under the armpits. I'll give him credit, he was strong! I'm no fly weight. Out I was. He was gradually cracking my ribs. The fish was still on. The logs were still coming. So was strong language. The legs began to tingle. Joy, oh joy!

The fish started downstream. Did you ever try to run with both legs asleep? I staggered to the challenge. The logs kept coming! "Keep your rod tip down!" Here was the great triumph of mind over matter, the legs started to work normally! For fifteen minutes I ran up and down that sand bar. I never gained line and never had to give it. The damned fool fish, with one jump, could have ended all! I never escaped from the dipsy doozy problem of keeping the line under the logs.

By this time both the guide and I were on non-profane speaking terms. We were both puzzled. We knew I had a good fish. We knew it was well hooked. That was the limit of our knowledge. Maybe it wasn't a fish. We also learned it was tiring. The care intensified with the lesser emergency. The guide had his net. The fish was in it. Take no chances! Get to the center of the sand bar! Empty the net! There in all his glory was the gentleman jackass, jumpingest so and so of a seven pound plus landlocked salmon!

Frustration

THE HOUSATONIC IN CONNECTICUT is a big river. It is generally wide around Cornwall Bridge; sometimes deep, and usually fast with its share of deceptive holes. The great State of Connecticut apparently stocks the river heavily, figuring, no doubt, it can hold more votes and people and fish than lesser waters. The power company recognizes the advantages of such hydroelectric potentialities and periodically raises and lowers the water. So far as I know, they are gentlemen about it. Nobody has been suddenly engulfed by a six foot bore but they seem rather to kid the fishermen along. At least they did in those days. Maybe they kidded the fish also. I don't know but I have strong suspicions.

Like other waters, part of the river is inhabited by small mouth bass and part of it is inhabited by stocked trout. There was a day when Atlantic Salmon rushed madly up the river from the sea to increase their breed. Considerable research fails to disclose the truth of the old story that early apprentices under their indentures could only be fed salmon and trout so many days each week. The salmon were up against the multiplying human race and multiplying fishermen. They also lost.

Many years ago also, the great State of Connecticut had lesser intelligence and more rigorous regulations. The season for trout ended June 30th and the season for small mouth bass opened July 1st.

FRUSTRATION

My opinion at the time was that the best trout fishing came the end of June. So I lived in anticipation and snuck in a couple of days at that time.

The first day's experience set the tenor of the holiday. I'd located a good fish on the far side of the stream. It was too deep to wade across but I went as far as the waders permitted. It took a longer cast to reach the fish than I was normally capable of making. On about one cast out of four I could get a reasonable float. At last I found a way to get four feet nearer without swimming. This meant fifty fifty on the floats. The range was under control. The multiplied fishermen were not.

Down the opposite shore came another man. He carried a bait casting rod and his line had a spoon on the end of it. He saw me casting. He saw the fish rise again. He cast to my fish! It was hooked and reeled rapidly up the other bank! The rod was dropped and the fish taken off. I'd guess that about two pounds of trout was slammed on the stones and then stuffed in his creel. He walked downstream. If he'd crossed over later I might have served a jail term!

There was no other success with the trout, but on June 30th I managed to land a half dozen small mouth bass running from one to two and a half pounds. My integrity was superb. I put each and every one back, carefully holding the fish; carefully removing hook and carefully seeing that my little friends started their lives again easily and upright in the water. None of them said thanks.

Late that afternoon I telephoned the bank, checked my calendar and said, "I have got a chance to get some small mouth bass fishing tomorrow and I'll stay over a day and bring you back some fish." Never, never, never boast!

I slept like a baby and dreamed of small mouth bass. Now this is really deplorable because I prefer trout and really only go for others when trout are not available. After breakfast I checked over my tackle and waded into the waters of the

Housatonic where the power company was then in a mood of beneficence.

July first was a wonderful morning of fishing. There was action all the time. I left at noon to go back to the bank and things I understood. During the morning of July first I had put back six nice trout! All I had left was a tattered integrity!

A few years ago I found that the State of Connecticut had a more modern approach and, for a fee of $5.50, permitted its senior citizens to buy a fishing license good for life. On my sixty-fifth birthday, May 25, 1964, I hocked the family jewels and bought just such a license. It was carefully pinned to my fishing vest on that very same day. It is still there. I have not fished in Connecticut since I bought the license.

P.S. More research, read "The Gist of It," Outdoor Life, September 1967.*

* *Outdoor Life,* in its "The Gist of It" column of September 1967, ran the following story of Bob Bolton, picked up from the *New Haven (Conn.) Register:* "REJECTION SLIP. One day in my travels around the state I stopped on a bridge and peered at several small trout in the pool below. The only thing I had in the car for enticement was the state's weekly fishing report. I tore off a piece of the paper and dropped it in. A trout swam up, sucked it in, and promptly spit it out. Not even the fish will swallow it."

The Light Still Flickers in the Window

FOR OVER TWENTY-FIVE YEARS I fished the Schoharie Creek with Art Flick and, may I add, learned mightily therefrom. Art is no spring chicken but he certainly gets around like one. My few extra years don't permit me to do so. At times he is really a demon fisherman. It's not that he doesn't put back more than his share, but because he goes at it with the enthusiasm of a ten year old and the experience and knowledge of Methuselah.

This last year we had a week together fishing the Connecticut River and tributary streams around the Connecticut Lakes in New Hampshire. The water was high and there were no ifs, ands, or buts about it. The lakes were full and while the power company normally lets out water during the night and shuts it off in the morning, we couldn't see any difference in the flow of the river at any time. It was always up. The water according to local fishermen was two feet higher than normal. I found one beautiful, long, swinging pool with steady current, protecting bank and adequate depth. I waded out well above my knees onto what was a normally dry sandbar and started to fish carefully from tail to head. In spite of this, I managed to snag a couple of small ones and when I rejoined Art, found he had been doing some exploring. His comment was, "You remember that couple we saw last night way out in the middle of nowhere?"

"Yep."

"Well, I have discovered how to get there. Let's go back after lunch and I'll try and drag you out there, but it's tough."

For once a fisherman had made an understatement. That afternoon we went back. We parked the car. This is where Indian Stream joins the Connecticut. The Indian at this point is a slower river. When they are lumbering up country, it is muddy and it seems to slobber all over the landscape when joining the Connecticut. We climbed down the bank. Art said, "Have you got your waders as high as you can pull them?" So I pulled again and tightened the suspenders.

"What's next?"

"I would suggest you follow close behind me. We've got about fifteen feet that are lousy. You'll approach the top of your waders and if you slip, it's just too bad!"

This was really comforting, as was his next comment, "Furthermore, the bottom is mucky and there are a lot of branches there so don't trip."

This was as close as I want to come to a heart attack! But clenching my teeth firmly, I refused his offer to carry my rod, took my life in my hands and said, "Proceed, Mr. Flick, proceed."

He had not understated the circumstances. I didn't yell for help; I didn't grab him by the back of the neck. I did follow in his footsteps. I did feel first one foot and then the other suck out of the muck. He spoke of branches. They were logs! I heaved. I trembled. I took out my ruler and the water was within 3/32 of an inch of the top of my waders! I did not know what cometh next!

We made it and as we arrived in the waist-high water and firm bottom, I wondered to myself, will the power company raise this water any higher when we return? Can I get back through this horrible mess if I am weighted down with a dozen big fish? But the problems of life were not over. We still had three or four hundred feet to travel, mostly across and then up in order to fish the current on the opposite shore upstream from the slobbering Indian.

In the process we took a few small fish. As you may gather, my friend Flick moved faster than I did, but I panted to remain within an appropriate distance.

Suddenly the air exploded. The hills echoed. I learned a lot about the true potentialities of the English language. The river started running upstream on one side. Art was waving his arms and rod. Did you ever try ducking a fly held by some sort of creature two hundred feet away? I ducked four times in eight seconds! Temper, temper, and a couple of wows! This really startled me and I started back. There was no hope. Art caught me. I felt his hot breath on my neck.

"What happened?"

"The best trout of the week!"

"What happened?"

"XX@###! ! ! The best Brownie of the year!"

"Did he get away?"

"X-X-X-@-#-#-# ! ! !"

"Now look here Art, what did happen?"

There was a very very long and very very pregnant silence. I used it to drop ten feet behind. My instinct was confirmed with his comment. He could not have looked me in the eye at that particular moment. Here was a really great fisherman saying, "He rose slowly. I saw him and like the rankest of beginners, worse by far than you Ogden, I took it away from him! I just barely pricked his lip!"

Brother, now I understood! Brother, he's human again! Brother, even the real pros, not just me, can do stupid things! He was just like the rest of us after all! He was a man!

"Let's go home. I'll get him tomorrow. I want a drink!"

"Sure."

I was grinning like a Cheshire cat and was saying nothing. I really don't think I'm a sadist at heart, but I don't even remember going through the muck on the way back!

That night it rained. The river rose some more and became dirty. We fished the small streams as best we could in the morning. It continued alternately to drizzle and rain. Art was silent. You could see his heart wasn't in it. A hatch seemed to be in the making.

"Let's go back. I want to catch that fish."

"O.K."

The car was parked in a pull-off on the far side of the road. We got out and crossed. The water looked muddy and was. Art started down the bank to face the horrible fifteen feet. Wisdom struck me smack in the puss.

"Art, I'm going to stay here, meditate, watch, maybe drive around, but at least keep dry."

There were a few mumbles that I'm sure were highly uncomplimentary. Today I am positive I was right! He struggled and to my surprise, made it. He certainly was of sound body if not mind. His churning legs set up bow waves and a slick behind. Laugh that one off! He almost made it. A hundred feet more to go and I saw him stand still, start his arm waving exercise and then faint laughter. Something was wrong. He was laughing! I went nearer to get a view of the upper river and there, going over his trout, was a fleet of seven canoes! Were you ever so tired you laughed? Were you ever so frustrated, disgusted, and mad that it made you laugh?

Art started back. The canoes went ashore about a quarter mile downstream. Art would periodically stop, shake his head and laugh. He floated through the frightful fifteen feet on pure laughter. He stopped and looked up at me thirty feet above him.

"Can you guess what the lead canoe asked me?"

"No."

"Mister, have you seen the school bus? I thought he was kidding and asked if they ran up and down the river. He was serious and said they were meeting it. Can you tie that?"

"Certainly Art, it's parked right behind our car with trailer for the canoes." The next day we went home, but the light still flickers in the window.

THE WEST

The West

AS WE MATURE, assuming application, hard work, some intelligence and a lot of luck, our economic background strengthens. Still relying on this tremendous assumption, our responsibilities and our ambitions also change.

In the case of fishermen, it is apt to find them improving their sportsmanship, putting back more and more smaller fish and, if they don't turn into fishers for big ones only, they are also inclined to fish more carefully where the big ones are. This may mean travel. They are also apt to pass up small rises. This may mean they miss some big ones, for a dimple can be extremely deceptive. Their fishing becomes more thoughtful. There is less racing from dawn to dark. The time and place are chosen and planned. I don't think anticipation lags, but rather that the urge to fish meets different needs.

With bigger responsibilities at the office and the drive for bigger fish, it has frequently happened that when problems arose, when fatigue hit hard, when boredom palled, or when inspiration was needed, I've gone fishing. The day or two became a week or longer. This has served the bank, my health and ability and, I believe, generally profitably. I recall very few major business decisions which were not influenced by or decided while fishing. It certainly cut down on the cigarettes; and that wonderful thing-a-ma-jig the "subconscious" kept plugging right along, clarifying and giving perception to everything, even trout. Wouldn't it be nice if we all had six subconscious thing-a-ma-jigs instead of a harried brain?

The Eton Collar

IN MY DAY, boys of nine went to Sunday school every Sunday. A cottage for the summer on a Wisconsin lake made no difference. It was considered proper to wear an Eton collar on Sundays. This was not because a boy so desired. It was because he had not yet won this obnoxious struggle. In addition, he walked a mile to Sunday school and stayed for church.

One Sunday in early July, when "the weather makes the corn grow," I was started off. I didn't hurry. There was little incentive. There was no smooth pavement; only a dirt road. It was nicer to walk in the heavy dust than in the grass and weeds at the roadside. Boys of nine don't fundamentally care how their shoes look. An occasional horse and buggy stirred up some dust. It was interesting to watch one come and go. Tim passed. The last quarter mile had to be stepped up a bit, or else. This means perspiration or sweat, take your pick.

Sunday school proceeded as expected. The family was met in front of the church. We walked down the aisle together. The church was crowded. Sometimes a restless boy, a hot church, a morning's walk and an Eton collar can blend into a truly amazing conglomeration. Parental glances stole my way. I continued to sweat. Maybe a horse had gotten mixed up in the amalgamation. It felt as if one was reclining beneath the collar. The parents had a whispered conference. My father leaned over and whispered that I could leave before the sermon if I cared to.

Would I! The trip back was done in half time. On arrival at the cottage, the irresistible attraction was the dock, the lake, and all things in the water. I was alone. There was no guardian of Sunday finery or Eton collars. Out on the dock I went, and flat on my stomach also. I had to examine just everything the water might offer. Wonder of wonders! Prize beyond compare! There, at the end of the dock, was the biggest rock bass the great State of Wisconsin ever produced. My nine-year-old heart made the elderly planks and pilings shudder. The bass looked friendly. Something had to be done!

During the preceding week I had been coached daily "don't scare the fish." This much had sunk in, and it must have taken considerable coaching. "My rod" was back at the bungelow, so I tiptoed off the dock and ran!

Where was the rod? Where was a hoe, or a spade or trowel? Where were the worms? A can of worms can turn to spaghetti in the sun. They had, and were dumped on the front porch. Mother's garden trowel was found in the kitchen. Into the garden in front of the porch I went like a bulldozer. There was nothing here, or here! By the water spout a small worm was cut in half! Both halves were grabbed. Another wrecking operation on a clump of grass alongside. The worms into the can. The trowel replaced the worms. The rod—oh yes, Dad told me to leave it behind the house.

That rod was chosen by myself to hold the fish of my dreams. The butt was large and solid. The ferrules were nickled brass, and decorated. The guides could hold a clothesline. It was hoisted over my shoulder and away we went! In a blaze of glory? I don't know, but one small boy, well lubricated by sweat, dirt and the supreme rapture of excitement known only to small boys, was off to destiny!

The lake's approaching a mile a minute. The heart is two

feet ahead of the feet. Downhill we go and naturally over we go too! The rod's not even bent; the worms are regathered, and all together we brake in a cloud at the dock. No one ever told me if they saw smoke, but I wouldn't be surprised.

"Don't scare the fish!" I whispered. Off with the shoes—too

noisy. A stealthy prowl to the end of the dock. I carefully lowered myself, Eton collar and all, to the dock without even a bounce on my tummy! The fish was still there. He seemed as friendly as ever. The restraint was enormous! The rod lay beside me. The bait was attached and the line was lowered hand over hand directly in front of this enormous prize. He looked, and liked, and took! I pulled, and hooked. Up I bounced and ran off the dock, fish, line and rod airborn behind me. I'm certain the rod bent like a 2 ounce bamboo. The knuckles of both chubby hands must have been white with the pressure. My speed was greater than the unwinding "crank-case." No chances could be taken on shore either! Up the bank, where the fish in flight made a one point landing! The rod was dropped. No pro football player ever made such a flying tackle of a slippery fish, and no such tackle was ever completed with the fish against the Eton collar!

Up the hill to the cottage and the returning family with the rod bumping along behind. My father disengaged the hook. Nothing was said about the dried worms on the front porch. My mother understood that a huge rock bass tasted better than chicken for Sunday dinner. Nothing was said about the garden or the trowel. No food, including the head and tail, ever tasted so good! That night, my father and I fished for bullheads and I got pricked. Also, I never again wore an Eton collar. Manhood had arrived.

Bugaboo

The bankers' skins were lily white
Every morning, noon and night
When with bugs they faced a trial
They won by an even country mile!

OUR FISHING PARTY was composed of four people. Two were very astute bankers. We took a float trip down the White River in Arkansas. Our two companions were experienced fly fishermen by normal standards. The Rainbows and the occasional Brownie in this river were good by any standards.

The river was beautiful in early July, clear and cold, as I am told it is throughout the summer. As the water comes out of the bottom, not the top of Bull Shoals Dam, it is kept that way. While we found great charm and awayness from such things as telephones, taxes and meetings, nevertheless we could not be entirely divorced from the needs of civilization and other men. Late each afternoon the water flow was stepped up to turn the wheels, to make the power, to light the lights and cook the food that fed the folks, that lived in the houses that Jack built.

When you were wading and that hour came, you got out of the water. It became too deep for comfort. The sun was hot; the water was cold and the semi-canyon through which much of the river flows was not too wide. The result was fog. During the day, the direct rays of the sun really burned the exposed portions of our bodies. Instead of the normal late day and evening fishing, you headed for camp and the evening's relaxed enjoyment.

Camping on shore, or an island, with a fire, good food and standard libations was almost as good as fishing. The evenings were cool. We pulled the boats up high on the bank and staked them safely. We could hear the water continue to rise some more feet. Before an early bed, we again pulled the boats higher. During the night some of us, but not the bankers, acquired distinctions of sorts on the individualized portions of their respective carcasses. I am told that not even the cooling breeze nor the cold water permitted peace. As a banker, I really wouldn't know.

In the morning we awoke in the fog. The water was cold and the coffee strong. After a leisurely and nourishing breakfast, we found renewed energy to return the boats from high ground to the river. The people in the houses that Jack built would return our river, our breeze, and their hot sun. Once again we pursued old Salmo Irideus. He seemed ready, and in never ending supply. It was almost like going to the office from nine to five but a very improved variation of that routine.

There were four of us on this trip plus two guides and a cook. We all enjoyed the trip and each other's company. All hands were good guys. We even enjoyed each other's wit! The two bankers continued to enjoy themselves after leaving the river. The other two fishers may have been very important. Whether they served as decoys has never been really determined. However, a certain hot shot engineer, burdened with degrees and specializing in highly technical valves, cutoffs, and clean rooms said he had collected a bright red ring around his equator, made up of numerous bites. Cutoffs were suggested. His response was some picturesque phrases. The vocal valves were all in good working order. The stream was suggested as a substitute clean room. It was cold and had no soothing effect on body or mind. He tried hard. Jupiter has a limited number of moons around its equator. He recognized no similarity and Jupiter was consigned to outer space—rather permanently. Atomic energy seemed to radiate from the mid section.

The other noble member of the quartet had a Ph.D. in Bio-Chemistry and his business was essential oils. I have never asked whether oil of citronella was an essential oil or whether oil is essential. It has not been determined whether he used some juice of his own concocting or whether he was just juicy. He certainly "lent flavor" to our party. Also the distribution was different. There was no concentration but malevolent spots, here, there, and everywhere. No great proportion, but no wide open spaces either. This was harder to treat. A good cummerbund would have protected the engineer from scratching. This man would have to have been mummified! A hospital checkup seemed in order. Both have recovered nicely and are doing well today in fishing, health and normal conversational achievement.

We bankers are deeply grateful for their charm and most useful company. If they willingly served as decoys, we still appreciate their heroism. Maybe it is just that bankers have both stamina and purity. In any event, we are grateful.

I've always dreaded black flies!
Mosquitoes are decently understanding!
Chiggers are discriminating feeders!

P.S. If all fishermen would agree, as we did, that spreading tin cans and garbage around campsites will spoil a beautiful river, then I might be able to persuade engineers and chemists to go again and to further assist the bankers in their Ph.D. thesis entitled "The Chigger Theory as Related to Bankers and Others."

We Live and Learn
First Lesson (A.M.)

MY WIFE AND I spent a few days at a small delightful dude ranch in Wyoming. It had a superb setting, about seven thousand feet up and surrounded by much higher mountains. There were, in addition, twenty-four nice people. The necessary number of horses were available and I neither know or care whether they were nice. Through the ranch ran a stream some thirty feet across and in the stream were trout. Also into and out of that stream ran irrigation ditches.

The wide open spaces, the western sky,
Can be better described by another guy!
The snow-clad crests
And timbered slopes
Are things reserved for other dopes . . .
I wanted to fish.

Our first day after arrival started with the acquisition of knowledge and ended with adventure. After breakfast, my wife looked over everything and everybody. I inquired about the stream and was directed to a path leading upstream. On arrival I learned that others had been similarly directed. It developed and was subsequently proven that there was only one other person at the ranch who knew anything about trout. The trout were there and so were the fisherwomen. The stream was very pretty—so were some of the women. One blond babe stood out in more ways than one! She looked like a sister to her daughter! Romance didn't die with King Arthur or thereabouts. Let's call her Guinevere, not Persevere, although she was pretty determined at that. Daughter hadn't been around as much. She was distinctly secondary, so let's refer to her as Guinevere Junior. Their tackle was not bad; their efforts were awful!

The social amenities serve a purpose in life. It is also true that a newcomer, particularly, will enjoy himself more if amicable relationships are gracefully established with fellow guests. Gentlemen prefer friendly amenities. As I stood on the bank, deep in reverie and shocked beyond words with the horrible things that were going on, I was immediately faced with a challenge.

"Is this a good place to fish?"

"Yes, I think so." I had noted that mother and daughter were fishing the tail of the pool with trout rising in the head.

"Are we fishing the right way?"

Oh, brother! "Let me see if I can help." Instantly I christened myself Sir Gallahad, or Sir Lancelot, or the Old King himself, I didn't know which! It didn't matter, but brother, she was Guinevere! A person less kindly disposed toward Bigelow might say I seized an opportunity to show off.

"Please may I see your rod?" I never saw a fly tied on sideways with one inch of gut sticking out before!

"Isn't it nice, you brought your nail clippers!"

Guinevere Junior had to have the same treatment. There was no barb on her hook. They had two flies between them!

"Can't you put a new barb on?"

"No, I'm sorry. Keep the fly in the air and off the rocks behind you. Look, that fly has a barb—not on the rocks or my eye, ear, nose or throat!" I couldn't possibly give my attention to two blond barbarians at the same instant. In spite of legend, I'll bet Lancelot couldn't either! I put on one of mine I didn't like.

"Mr. Bigelow, how do you cast a fly?" cooed Guinevere Senior.

Back to the early days. "Lift the fly from the water like so," said I motioning with my rod. "When the rod reaches 12 o'clock, let the line straighten out behind you. Feel its weight—I mean the line, Guinevere, not yours! Bring the rod forward as if you were driving a nail with a hammer." I made several casts which, for illustration at least, were perfect. "Now," I said, "take this handkerchief (thank heaven I had a clean one) and hold it in your armpit while you cast. Let's take a short line first, I'll hold your hand."

"Guinevere, you're too damned strong! Let your hand relax at least! But before we do that let's look at the fly again! You don't fish behind you, you fish in front—keep the fly in the air! All right, here we go again. That's fine! That's fine! Now we've got the fly in the air front and back and this time we'll cast. Whoopsie do!"

A No. 12 fly made a splash like a boulder. "Not so hard!"

"But I thought you said hit it like a hammer!"

"Yes, madam, but not like a pile-driver!"

"O.K." "Mr. Bigelow you're hurting my hand!"

"I'm sorry! Now you're getting the hang of it. Now look, Guinevere, we've been practicing casting. Look out, you dropped the handkerchief!"

Her grab was quicker than mine and she popped it into her bosom. My hand had followed all the way from the ground. It stopped within a quarter inch! I shook! She did not! Who was fishing for what? I don't know whether trout rise this way or not. Anyhow somebody was damn near caught! Who? Don't ask me! I nearly screamed anyway. All right, cancel out one handkerchief! Thank goodness my nose wasn't running even if my mind was!

Let's try the head of the pool. There are fish rising up there, do you see them?"

"You knew those fish were here all the time. You're wonderful!"

That was the real sales pitch!

"All right, let's move quietly and get up so that we can cast this fly a few feet ahead of that fish that's rising."

"Why do you cast ahead of the fish?"

"So it will float down just as if it was a natural insect."

"Can those fish tell the difference?"

"Tell the difference between what?"

"A natural insect and a fly."

"Sometimes they can, that's what we try to avoid!" I was wondering whether I had a beginner, an old pro or a natural. Into neutral again. So Guinevere Junior got the word.

"Come and join us!"

"Not so fast for the love of Heaven, and don't walk through the pool!"

"I'm sorry!"

I turned back to Guinevere Senior. "All right, let me have your hand again and relax Guinevere, relax. Now we're getting the line out." My hand reached over her shoulder on her hand, the line was getting out and she was watching my face! King Arthur was stern as hell!

This time the king was stronger than Guinevere. This time my hand was not objectionable. The first cast hooked the first fish.

"What do I do now?"

"Turn the handle on the reel!"

She turned it in the right direction and kept on cranking. The line shrank and the poor fish couldn't help himself anymore than I could! Finally I shouted, "Hold everything! Back up please!" I'll be damned if she didn't, with the trout two feet from the tip of the rod!

She was jubilant!

I was exhausted!

After appropriate admiration I suggested the pool be rested before Guinevere Junior was turned loose. Everybody knew everything, so I got out while the getting was good! Also I needed a rest!

As I slowly ambled upstream, I found that where each irrigation ditch poured back into the stream there was a small pool. While they watched, I took three trout from three ditch entrances, all within their sight. My ego was recovering rapidly.

As you may imagine, luncheon showed I had made the grade as a fisherman. I was a great authority and a local hero for the moment. This is one way to get a reputation if you want to earn it the hard way.

"How do trout like worms?" "Are irrigation ditches better than trout streams?" "We must do it again!"

It was an only human temptation to take up embroidery and tell, amidst waving arms, some really tall stories. I was almost convinced that I was a hero. I started to tell about the big fish that got away just at dark. My wife interrupted. Every time I started to tell a new story, my wife interrupted. God bless her! If she had not, I might have told the story of the prehistoric trout and I am certain they would have swallowed the whole piece of driftwood. Here was a chance of a lifetime to show off!

It finally dawned on me that she meant to interrupt. Well, anyway she did. It was just as well because the afternoon story was believed; and it was true, from beginning to end!

We Live and Learn
Second Lesson (P.M)

DID YOU EVER SEE A DOG that was seventy-five percent golden retriever and the balance the State of Wyoming? I have. He was a beautiful, big, friendly fellow and furthermore well trained, in more ways than one.

That afternoon, exhausted from my morning's experiences, I took a nap. When I woke up there was no one around—not even my wife. She likes horses; I like fish. I subsequently learned that my wife's horse of the day had the cozy habit of trying to lie down in the stream. This is not good for fishing. I haven't the slightest doubt in the world that the horse learned what I have known for years.

Back to the events of the day. In an emergency one should go fishing. I got into my clothes and, thinking of the morning, headed down the stream. As I passed the corral, this beautiful big, friendly fellow shook his legs also. He had four. I have two. He was better at it and all four feet pushed him into the air. Also, as we went down the road, I learned he was not only trained to walk behind but, being a good politician as well as a canine genius, would occasionally lick my hand! I thought it must be admiration. Whether it was the golden retriever or the State of Wyoming that was predominant I didn't know.

We headed through the woods and he still trailed along,

calm, collected, friendly and well trained. We got to the stream and I went in. He followed me in, but again he stayed behind me as I started fishing up to the ranch.

The fishing was gorgeous. There was no one—let alone blond, around. I was nearly always able to wade the center and fish both sides as well as the middle. There was no back cast problem. My casts always stay in the air! Therefore there was no problem of a hare's ear or a dog's ear, only my own ear. Each bend, each fallen tree, each run seemed to provide a fish. The kitchen had told me their icebox was full, so for two hours I revelled in catching twelve to fifteen inch trout and an occasional one a bit larger. They all went back. It was all beautiful! The day was beautiful; the stream was beautiful and I was happy enough to think that maybe some of it might rub off on the Bigelow physiognomy!

Once in a while I'd hear a splash behind me. But I wasn't being interfered with and the trout, the birds, some small wild life along the stream and the complete solitude left me with nothing but contentment. The fish were coming so well that I must have put back several dozen. It seemed that I could practice casting over live fish and the game became one of catching them, not for the sake of the catch, but to do it artistically. The contrast couldn't possibly have been greater between the morning and the afternoon exercise. I always did like the second lesson best, it was that much nearer the end.

At long last, and it seemed like minutes, I arrived back opposite the ranch and there I saw the horses and riders returning. Stopping in mid-stream to watch and greet them, I heard a real splashing in the water behind me and turned around for the first time to see what my companion was doing. There he was, rushing madly back and forth in six inches of water. He was obviously chasing something or possibly trying to keep something from getting back to the main current and deeper water.

Whatever his objective, it failed and he actually joined me! As mine host and his attendant party rode up I asked, "Is it possible that this dog goes fishing?" The answer was, "He certainly does! He's brought a dozen trout to the ranch house so far this year!"

I saw and believed and learned something new in the month of July 1963! Here was a real dog, twenty-five percent golden retriever and seventy-five percent trout fisherman!

"Legal Trout"

YOU PROBABLY THINK that what I am writing about is either six or seven inches long. You couldn't possibly be more wrong. I have nothing of this nature in mind, although the thought occurs that I thoroughly like the new approach of many Conservation Departments, that you must keep the fish that is hooked, regardless of length. Actually I have been sort of puzzled about those streams where you can't keep fish under twelve or fifteen inches. The purpose of both regulations is important, but if we applied the same philosophy, it would not accomplish the purpose. It's all very confusing; therefore, I would like to repeat again that the title of this story has nothing whatsoever to do with the exigencies of these situations.

Once upon a time, there was a spring-fed stream far up in the north country. The water temperature was always, winter and summer, fifty-five degrees. The water level rarely changed an inch and even when the winter winds blew and the thermometer plummeted clear to hell and gone, the stream never froze over. It remained fifty-five degrees.

Now this stream was loaded with trout—several kinds. In the dim historical era, when this story starts, there were a few people there with large Victorian estates and the same thing is true today. It is loaded—I mean the stream, and probably, periodically, some of the people. The only way to reach it is through a couple of roads that cross it or through private estates. Frankly, if I owned property on this wonderful stream, I would also have available several shotguns loaded with rock salt. This at times can have an exhilarating effect on poachers. How do I know—never mind!

But to get back to the subject, once upon a time a man with a lot of dough bought up a good many thousand acres immediately adjacent to this water. It was all part of the same spring-fed valley. Along the side of the stream he put up a great dam, made of muck, so that he could keep his little fishies all to himself. No doubt it was in keeping with the regulations of the times, because that dam varied from six to seven inches in height. This doesn't have anything to do with legal trout either.

I have a friend who is older than I, and who learned to fish this water as a boy. I never thought it would be courteous to ask if he ever did any poaching, so I cannot give you the answer. However, as he grew to manhood, death came to the man who had accumulated this wonderful preserve and the property was sold.

The new owner was undoubtedly a better fisherman than the poor fellow who went to his reward. The reason I say this is that he rarely paid any attention to anything else, and his catches of denizens of this piscatorial paradise were undoubtedly greater by far than his acquisition of material wealth. Life for him had two potentials, one pleasant and the other making ends meet. Being human, he gave his attention to catching fish and, when necessary, avoiding the sheriff. After one period of furtive existence, he sought out my friend. Both had undoubtedly been fishing together many times, and both were born to the country. One had spent a little more time accumulating the world's goods. The poor devil who thought only of the finer things of life asked for help.

I really don't know anything about this discussion, but a loan of one thousand dollars was made and, as the lender

believed that some evidence of responsibility should be given "for the good of the owner," it was duly decided that a lien would be taken on the trout within this empoundment. Therefore a mortgage document was drawn up. It said that, "The Grantor, does give, grant, bargain, sell and confirm unto said Grantee all those fish contained within these premises. More fully described on a certain map entitled .... and filed in the Office of the Town Clerk, reference thereto being had for a more particular description of said premises." This was an impressive document. I am certain it ended up with *et al.*, *et ux* etc. I am also certain that both men fished happily together for some years and caught and ate and released a great many trout that were large, very large and tremendous. I don't dare guess how many and how large, even though I have been there. You wouldn't believe me anyway. You would be completely wrong.

Three men can recall one blistering summer day at three o'clock in the afternoon where no fish under fourteen inches was caught by any of us. We also recall that every time one of fourteen to eighteen inches was hooked, a dozen submarines came up from the depths to look the victim over. It was then I first saw an albino trout—two of them in fact, both at least thirty inches long! It's a nice place to fish. I'd like to try it in the evening.

It was this sort of thing that in due course took the second owner to his reward. He must have died very happily, a smile on his face; his dreams coming true; his pockets empty and perhaps his bills unpaid. I couldn't think of a better way to spend one's declining years than to fish cold water and wild country for sizable trout with good company. Maybe he considered he was in Heaven then. If I get to the same place in due course, I will ask him.

At any rate, the man who lent the money undoubtedly pondered his deceased friend's problems and his own future fishing potential. He did not worry about his thousand dollar mortgage, in fact, he had forgotten the money when he made the deal. Most of the winter was spent in this way, and in due course the willows showed the breath of spring and the skunk cabbages got restless. My friend did likewise when the postman delivered a letter from an eminent firm of lawyers in a great metropolitan area. Their subtlety was equalled by their tender loving care, as set forth in their letter which appeared somewhat in the following spirit:

LEGAL TROUT

BLANK, BLANK AND ANOTHER BLANK
Attorneys at Law
Metropolitan Center

Dear Sir:

It would appear from the land records of . . . . . locality that you hold what purports to be a mortgage on the fish within the property of the late John Doe. This instrument is both ridiculous and useless.

We have a client who intends to purchase this property and we wish it discharged for the record. Please have a discharge prepared and forward it to us promptly.

Very truly yours,

I asked my friend, "What did you do?"

The answer was, "Put it in the basket."

"Then what happened?"

"Well, in a couple of weeks I got another letter which ran about as follows:

BLANK, BLANK AND ANOTHER BLANK
Attorneys at Law
Metropolitan Center

Dear Sir:

We attach a copy of letter written you two weeks ago. We have had no answer. The instrument is worthless.

Please consult your attorney and send discharge immediately. We wish to close the title shortly.

Very truly yours,

"What did you do?"

"Same thing."

"Well?"

"Same basket."

"Then?"

"Well, a week or so later I got a telephone call. They asked me if I was the man who owned a crazy mortgage on some fish. I said I was. They asked if I had received their letter and I said 'Yep.' They asked if I had answered the letter and I said, 'Nope.' They wanted to know what I had done with the letters and I told them. They allowed as how they wanted to talk to me and I allowed as how I didn't want to talk to them. I could hear some whispering and then, 'How much would I want to discharge this worthless instrument?' The answer was 'Nothing.' This answer really delayed the game! 'Well, what did I want?' Now it was my turn to be stumped but I said I wanted to talk to the buyer. It was then carefully explained to me that they represented the buyer. They had his power of attorney and full authority to act.' "

"Well, what did you say to that?"

"I told them it was fine by me, wished them a Happy New Year and said goodbye. The fishing season hadn't arrived yet anyway so why should I get into a sweat?"

"All right, all right, but what the hell happened?"

"Well, a few days later the telephone rang and when I answered it I heard, 'I'm the guy who is trying to buy the property where you have a mortgage on the fish. My attorneys seem hot and bothered and tell me you would like to talk to me. I will be in your town day after tomorrow—how about it?"

"Sure, glad to."

"What time?"

"Suit yourself—will be here all day."

"About ten O.K.?"

"Fine."

"Brother, you changed your tune!"

"Well, he sounded like a nice guy in spite of his lawyers."

"Did he show?"

"Sure."

"What happened?"

"Well, he said, 'You seem to have my lawyers all teed off. You don't seem to have horns—what's the score?' "

"What did you tell him?"

"Well, I told him the story of how I had been given the mortgage; that I had enjoyed fishing this water for over fifty years, and that I never had and did not expect to get my money back. He started grinning and then asked me, 'What should I say?' I told him that if he would simply tell me that when he or his guests were not at his lodge, then I could go in with an occasional friend. With this statement I'd see he had his discharge before he left town."

"His hand came out with the words, 'Let's have a drink.' We did, in fact we each bought one at ten thirty A.M. And that, Ogden, is how you got here today."

My friend is at least ten years my senior. I have since obtained an introduction to the owner. When I go through next—if I do—it would be more important even than the fish to see both these very very refreshing guys.

Reading the Bottom

SINCE SOME FISHERMEN fished with a fly, since some of them wrote articles and books, since most of them appeared human, there has been a constant discussion of the merit of wet vs. dry flies. This is often started in the early morning, which is the time to sleep, and continues far into the night, which is also the time to sleep. It goes with all sorts and kinds of technicalities, whether you twitch or double twitch; whether you use a 2, 4, 6, 8 or 10 tippet; the temperature of the water, drag, dressing and all the rest.

It may be oversimplification, and it certainly does dispense with a lot of conversational fringe benefits, but nevertheless, it does seem to me that there are just two branches of fly fishing. One is dry and the other is wet. I would agree that Bucktails and nymphs are arts in themselves, but the only reason I would question their being classified as wet fly fishing would be that nymphs take extraordinary keen eyes, sensitive hands and a psychic gift. This sort of distinction, if it doesn't make the world go 'round, at least helps man to justify fishing again, and again, and again. Mostly this improves the disposition of the man and the happiness of the family for short periods of time.

Somebody, however, is always noted for bringing up the type of cast and how it should be executed. The speed of the water, whether or not a floating or sinking line is a requisite, the length of leaders, and I think of twenty, thirty or forty feet, all add to the mess. These things can be overdone. Some of our more gifted conversational purists say that each approach has its individual time, place and techniques. Certainly they have more knowledge and experience than I.

Still, in my own very humble way, I think that wet and dry fly fishing can be further lumped together by one grand philosophy—learn to read the bottom. This does not necessarily mean that for a rushing trout stream one should acquire a glass bottomed boat. I didn't say to look at the bottom—I said learn to read it. This is more effective than taking knots out of leaders or sitting on a rock to wait for the swallows, and it has been known to produce fish.

Now I am fundamentally a dry fly man, but extraordinarily a couple of the best catches I have ever had were kneeling on the bank and fishing a wet fly upstream, or fishing a Bucktail upstream on a short line in a brown flood. Somehow either the flies or the Bucktails on those occasions seemed to cover the right bottom at the right time, at the right depth, at the right speed, and with the right twitch or double twitch.

Did you ever watch a water snake fish upstream at mid-day in crystal clear, shallow water? Did you notice how he fastened his tail on a good rock and poked his nose under the rocks upstream? I like this approach to fishing. Human ingenuity is wonderful. It's like the ferry across the Snake River south of Jackson Hole. You drive your car onto a barge. There are two ropes across the stream. The barge is at an angle and the river pushes the barge across. It's the same thing. You let someone else do your work for you. Now if you read the bottom, your trout get the idea. Furthermore, you will probably catch fish if you read it well.

As a matter of fact, you can fish all sorts of ways. Have you ever let your line trail over your shoulder while you light a cigarette and have some damned fool trout seize a sodden dry fly and make you waste a match and a cigarette? That dry fly didn't find the bottom all wet.

It comes back to my favorite—the dry fly. Now here is real art. Here is something my friends and enemies alike say I know something about. They don't say how much. I don't care for I go my own way and always try to read the bottom. This matching the hatch stuff is bunk. It makes good reading when somebody knows how to write. Why do I say this? How do you match a hatch if there ain't no hatch? I can tell you, read the bottom.

I recall one Christmas week, snow on the ground, ice on the stream and absolutely no flies hatching. Sometimes even flies are smart. I read the bottom, fished a dry fly, furthermore took six fish in the short two hours before dusk. I read the bottom. If you are getting nasty about the foregoing statements, I was about to say that it was a club "put and take" stream that hadn't been stocked since July. To get nastier myself, I had a friend with me who fished wet. He didn't read the bottom. He didn't catch any fish. He saw me catch my fish. He's dead. You have just got to learn to read the bottom to know where the fish lie.

Did you ever have the experience of seeing a pool full of fish rising or dimpling or swirling just below the surface and not being able to do business? Did you try a dry fly first? Did you change dry flies? How many more times than once? Did you change the size of your hooks? Did you go down to No. 20s? Did you try a Fan Wing Royal Coachman on a No. 8 hook? Did you catch any fish? Do you know anything more exasperating?

Did you switch to wets? Did you fish the 45° angle? Did you try it upstream? Fast? Slow? Was the wet any better than a dry? Tell me, did you use just a teeney weeney bit of lead? Did you ever experience anything more exasperating? Did you read the bottom?

One more question, were there any fish in the creel at any time? Of course there weren't—you didn't read the bottom; neither did the fish! How could anyone catch trout without reading the bottom? They can't—that's definite and final. Just how do you read the bottom? Go stick your head in the water! P.S. Polaroid glasses help!

ABROAD

Fields Abroad
or
The Declining Years

THERE ARE STILL DREAMS of the fish that got away, the ones seen but not even pricked and the hope of new experiences and additional joys to be acquired in a more sedate manner. This I am living through and loving every minute. The streamside life has become more personal and can be enjoyed without pressure. A mother merganser and her eight ducklings running across the top of a pool at the bend are every bit as thrilling as a giant trout. Even meeting different fishermen seems to soften the prejudices of a lifetime. While the sight is poorer, I am sure we see more and sometimes learn more too. It took me many many years to learn there are times when a trout taking a sixteen or twenty fly should not be struck on the rise. He may require a few seconds. Why?

I would like to go back to Norway when the sea trout are running. I would like to bathe my soul again in the Test or some other English stream. For that matter, I would like to watch their crazy voles.

In Chile there will always be the challenge of the big fish, but what about the winds of the Argentine? Also, I would like to see some of the red deer of England that are now crossing the Andes from Argentina to Chile. Spain and Portugal sound like gentlemen fishing. I have never been there but I would like to fish in Ireland, Scotland and New Zealand. I want to see their fish, their animals, their birds and their fishermen. When the times comes to cross the River Styx, I hope I may be granted a couple of hours to fish a Gray Fox Variant or a Blue Dunn (with natural hackle) quietly and reflectively—even if the waders leak.

By-Products

WE HAVE ALL HEARD the old clichè about the fishing trip where "some damned fool wanted to fish." We have also heard the answer to the question "Why do men go fishing?" given as "To catch fish." Those comments are probably true in all too many cases. Everybody has made one or more attempts to explain why men go fishing. The best reason I ever saw given was in Roderick L. Haig-Brown's book called *A River Never Sleeps*. It is the last paragraph of the last chapter. The last copy of many copies that I have bought had to be purchased at auction. I paid through the nose and again found it worth it.

Having given you a good research idea, I am certainly not going to lend my feeble efforts to an improvement attempt that would be impossible for me. The purpose of this yarn is solely to illustrate its title by telling you of some odds and ends of things that I have thoroughly enjoyed while ostensibly trout fishing. The incidents are totally disconnected. I also get that way at times.

* * *

The judge and I were casting the shore of a pond and hoping for the best. There was a big ruckus in the bushes with a couple of birds making a real to do. We paddled closer and heard something coming down the bank. We arrived simultaneously with the great grandpappy of bullfrogs. He had an almost fully grown catbird in his mouth! We swung a paddle, missed!

Grandpappy leapt at least thirty feet into the water and went to the bottom. The bird popped out, suffocated. The judge would bear witness in court.

* * *

In recent years we have all seen perfectly georgeous television pictures of animals both in black and white, and in color. As a result, many of us have watched that very playful animal, the otter. They do not see a fraction as well as they play or swim. It was my privilege to sit on a rock and watch a pair of them on a snow slide having the time of their lives. Maybe this is one of the reasons I have developed a belly. Bellies can be useful as well as entertaining. This sight was a by-product to remember. Let's go fishing again!

* * *

Have you ever seen that bird called a water ouzel? A good part of its diet is insect life from streams and it has the ability to walk around on the bottom under the water. Look it up in your bird book, which may or may not tell you that it is by nature and instinct a confirmed flirt. It goes popping in and out and always seems to stay just so far ahead. Bird watchers have multiplied almost as fast as fishermen and some of them are equally emphatic in their statements, whether true or untrue. I have a lot of friends who are bird watchers and presumably some of them know something about it. I have watched several water ouzels while fishing in the West and one, just one, in a local stream in Connecticut within four miles of my office. Some of the bird watchers believe me. I know I am right and to hell with the rest of them!

* * *

We are still trying to find out whether we go fishing to drink or catch fish, or at least I am trying to pinpoint some of the reasons I have gone fishing. The ones given here are those that are suitable for publication, and I am keeping the others to myself.

BY-PRODUCTS

* * *

As long as we are on the subject of birds, have you ever fished a stream and been repeatedly "buzzed" by a redwinged blackbird? The old lady probably had a nest on the bank and was not a believer in peaceful co-existence. It happens if you get too close. Well, if you haven't been buzzed, you have missed something which is quite entertaining. If you are less fortunate than I, you may have noticed however that same redwinged blackbird standing on a stone partially covered by water and picking insects off the wet part of the stone. Now I didn't catch this fish—I wish I had. But I saw a big eleven pound trout, a Brownie naturally. He had been caught in Wyoming and when opened up there inside his tummy was a freshly caught redwinged blackbird! All of this goes to show that a well-developed Brown Trout would like a good chicken dinner, and that the stupid blackbird isn't always baked in a pie.

* * *

Are you ready for more about Wyoming? My wife and I were driving through and stopped for the night at a nice motel in a small town. I followed the usual procedure of buying unnecessary tackle at the sporting goods store and said to the owner, "I have only got a couple of hours in the morning, have you any suggestions?" The answer was, "Why don't you try the stream which runs through the park around the corner?" I did, and the next morning took, and put back, my limit of decent trout from the Little Popo Agie as it passed through civilization. As we moved on, the stream went underground beneath a mountain, and when it came out, my wife had a wonderful time feeding crackers to the really big ones which were protected and viewed from a distance above. I have photographs of the wife, the trout and the crackers. It did not inspire me to go fishing in Central Park, New York City.

* * *

I don't always go fishing in parks, nor do I always fish in

Wyoming. Any gifts of which I may be possessed don't ordinarily run to the artistic. Nevertheless, a very large part of the fun of fishing is to observe what goes on while we struggle with ourselves and/or the fish. The most beautiful thing I ever saw on the stream happened not once but was repeated five times one morning on the Big Hole River in Montana. The part of the river I fished was a sort of a miniature of the Snake and we bounced along at a fast clip in a rubber raft built for two. The water was clear and cold and the banks were deeply wooded. When we swung around a bend there was often very fast water and my guide controlled the raft from the front so that I got each new vista and could keep my fly in the water or the air as much as I could. Imagine really fast water and a really sharp bend and looking straight ahead some thirty or forty feet, you see two great horned owls sitting on a branch and they are as surprised as you are. They don't drop from the branch, they don't jump from the branch, they float away from the branch in a silence so great you can feel it. Side by side with a combined ten foot wingspread, they cross the river in front of you. Someday I am going to be a bird watcher. This happened five times one morning and I'd love to see it again. There is still one more by-product to bring me out of the air and back to earth.

* * *

When my wife and I were finishing our holiday, we had a limited time to take that gorgeous drive from Duluth up the north shore of Lake Superior. I wanted to see the Nipigon. I had read about the world record brook trout. I didn't expect to have time to fish, but I wanted to see where such a revered Fontinalis came from. My visions of the river were totally wrong. It is not a stream but a big, wide beautiful outlet to a big, cold and beautiful lake. It wants to get to Superior and it wants to get there in a hurry. I watched at dusk and saw one man catch a good fish. He told me he had been coming at exactly this time every year for over twenty years. This I can understand. We went back to the motel. The old banker was happy. He had seen what he had wanted to see. The next day we would head for Port Arthur and the boat and the grand-children in Toronto.

* * *

Sleep was satisfying. We woke up early and as we had the time, thought it would be nice to drive from Nipigon down to the mouth of the river where it entered Lake Superior. We did so and looked over the little lumber port of Red Rock. It didn't take long and we had our drive ahead. When we got out of town and almost back to the main highway, there with his car across the road was one of the Royal Canadian Mounted Police. Naturally we stopped. Keeping his eye firmly upon me, except when he glanced at the license, he asked with their impeccable politeness, "You are from Connecticut?"

"Yes, sir."

"Are you an American citizen?"

"Yes, sir."

"Where were you born?"

"Evanston, Illinois."

"Where did you enter Canada?"

I told him.

"How long have you been here?"

"About three days."

"Where are you going?"

"Back to Port Arthur where we get the boat to see our daughter in Toronto."

"What are you doing in Canada?"

"Enjoying it and looking over the fishing country."

"Madam, you are Mrs. Bigelow?"

"I believe so."

"Where were you born?"

"Montclair, New Jersey."

"How old are you?"

She dodged this one. He thought she looked honest, so he said to me, "Please open the trunk."

"Certainly." So I got out, took the keys and walked around feeling as though I had a gun in my back. I opened the trunk. There were the bags, waders and fishing gear.

"All right, close it up. I'll let you go on."

I got safely back in my seat and said, "By the way, officer,

I have been to Canada many times and have always enjoyed it. My mother was a Canadian. I have never had this happen before. What is the reason?"

"Somebody robbed the bank early this morning."

* * *

Now you know why I like to go fishing. It's quite an adventure for a Sound Old Banker.

The First Grandchild

NOW THERE ARE SEVEN and two thirds. Four are my daughter's. My son has three. The first was my son-in-law's. This is quite an achievement! I don't care how good my son and his wife are, they will never catch up! They can't! My first grandchild was eaten! It's all very confusing. It was then. It still is. There never was such a child. It should go down in story if not song. It can't go in song—there are too many bass notes.

The first grandchild is worse than one's own first child. You worry twice as much. You worry for your child and your child's child. This makes twice. There are two grandparents, so you worry four times as much! You also feed on each other's worries, not on your grandchildren. We hadn't known that our daughter and son-in-law, who up to then we had loved so dearly, both had a canabalistic libido.

Relationships between parents and children and their fiancees are important. When my daughter informed me she was getting married, I started to raise the usual questions and was informed that he was a fisherman and a very good one! Politics had already started, so I thought I might as well join the game and asked him for a weekend fishing. He played politics too. That stymied the daughter. Who ever said an old dog can't learn new tricks? I guess I closed my eyes to the whole deal because he was really a pretty good fisherman, or at least talked like one.

They were married but not until the old man had provided his daughter with waders and wading brogues. I had the courage to decline a new rod as the prospective son-in-law had at least 376 already and I thought he should share something. Following the honeymoon, during which the parents recovered a portion of their equilibrium, the kids got into the car and left for Alberta. The only reason I have ever been able to figure why they went there was that the fishing was supposed to be pretty good. This guy walked into our lives, stole our daughter and went fishing! When I have had problems I have gone fishing too, but I haven't figured out yet where the problem was. Maybe we all had 'em. We all got political. At any rate, it didn't do me any good to figure.

After some months the proper thing to do, or maybe the selfish one, was to drive 2500 miles to see them. Dick and I went fishing. He took along a friend, probably for protection. As we strung up our lines, I made the comment to this fellow, "I have never fished in Alberta but I always start with one of Art Flick's Gray Fox Variants." The guy commented, "So do I," and he did, even though he had never seen the Catskills. I put him down as a better fisherman than Dick, but Dick caught the fish.

There's always a certain amount of kidding in this sort of deal. My comments on seven inch trout didn't go over very well. Wise parents gradually learn you can wear out your welcome with newlyweds. When we departed I left with them some barbed comments about the next stop, Lake Pend O'reille. I described in detail what kind of wires I would send collect after each big fish had been safely landed. Some of those needles sank in pretty deep. There was blood in the gutters. The trip was not very successful. You don't get the big fellows in the middle of the summer. They are down deep; so was I. Actually I didn't realize how deep I was in.

Modesty was forced back on my shoulders and we arrived

back home prepared for a placid winter. This is something that just doesn't happen. We were informed that our first grandchild would arrive in May. In November, the kids told us they were going on to Kamloops, British Columbia. I suppose they knew the fishing was better. They drove over the Big Bend. They didn't figure on a snowstorm. We were told about the trip with comforting descriptive remarks and my daughter

CLASS OF SERVICE

This is a fast message unless its deferred character is indicated by the proper symbol.

WESTERN UNION

TELEGRAM

W. P. MARSHALL, PRESIDENT

1956 FEB 1201 AM 5 4

SYMBOLS

DL=Day Letter

NL=Night Letter

LT=International Letter Telegram

The filing time shown in the date line on domestic telegrams is STANDARD TIME at point of origin. Time of receipt is STANDARD TIME at point of destination

=BA015

B RAA034 41 COLLECT NL=CPR FD KAMLOOPS BC 7=

=OGDEN BIGELOW=

3 GLEN COURT GREENWICH CONN=

=NEWEST ADDITION ARRIVED TWO PM THIS AFTERNOON AFTER ONLY THIRTY FIVE MINUTES LABOR WEIGHED IN AT EIGHTEEN POUNDS THIRTY SEVEN INCHES LONG NAMED IT STEELHEAD DADDY DOING WELL SAVING TWIN FOR YOUR ARRIVAL WILL PAY FOR LIKE NEWS FROM YOU=

THE COMPANY WILL APPRECIATE SUGGESTIONS FROM ITS PATRONS CONCERNING ITS SERVICE informed us that the child in due course would be named "Pretzel."

We had learned that you can't live your children's lives for them but we were still learning what your children can do to you. I think both of them were crazy! So we started worrying and continued it. The telephone bills those days were something and we began laying plans for a trip to Kamloops to give suitable greeting to the new arrival in May. After all, the first grandchild doesn't arrive every day.

One Sunday in March (seven months) the doorbell rang at about 6:30 A.M. The raucous noise shattered much-needed slumber. I think Western Union gave the wire the same interpretation I did! I rolled out of bed and staggered down the stairs holding the rail with one eye and both hands. I thought of the kitchen door, thought better of it, and finally swung open the front door. Would I accept a collect telegram? Where from? Kamloops. Yes, yes, and yes! I glanced at it, left the door open, ran upstairs and really shook my wife awake! While she was trying to focus on this masterpiece of iniquity, I read it a second time myself!

Then I had to apologize to my wife! Palsy stayed with me until eleven o'clock. My wife was then able to let me care for myself. She phoned the kids. Which one of those devils did it? How could they do such a thing? We have since wondered which one wanted the first steak or whether they had been cooking this grandchild together for seven months. Eighteen pounds and thirty seven inches combined with love and evil would furnish a lot of food. This was our first grandchild! They smoked it and ate it! This was horrible beyond T.V. and we never, I mean never, fully recovered!

We again headed west in May. My wife's arrival was timed to precede the blessed event. It was indicated that I would be in the way, so I stopped off at Qualicum Bay, Vancouver Island to go fishing. It was more fun. The company was quiet and considerate. After coming in one evening, we mixed some martinis in man-sized glasses. This also made sense and as I started to raise this delectable fluid to my sunburned puss, the telephone rang. I answered.

"It's a boy! Your first grandson has arrived! They're both O.K."

"Dick, you're a damned liar, it's the second!"

The martini was finished, also I vaguely recall another one just as large. I don't know yet whether grandchild number one or number two caused the greatest strain. If it hadn't been for number two, I would have smoked and eaten the parents!

The Second Grandson

MURDER WILL OUT. The boy is a fisherman. Neither his pappy nor his grandpappy can understand it. He has been bitten badly—and at an early age. Not by his parents or his grandfather either directly or indirectly, but by numerous fish.

There's such a thing as fisherman's luck, but there's also a thing such as learning how to fish. This kid's first experience was a three-and-a-half pound small-mouthed bass. I could never understand why his dad would take a boy of five-and-a-half years fishing, and then not help the kid land such a fish, but make him do it himself. This is bad; also I'm in favor of motherhood. I am told it didn't bother the boy a bit. That conceivably could be related to an iniquitous ancestry.

At any rate, the boy was bitten but good, and at every opportunity thereafter went fishing. The worst of it was that he seemed on every occasion to be successful, mostly with perch. There was no question that he always caught more fish than his brothers, or friends of his age. What was equally apparent was that he knew it.

Now every human should enjoy watching a small boy catch fish. His enthusiasm, concentration, and dedicated commitment are a joy to behold, and nearly every fisherman, seeing such a thing, lives over again his own catches and tries to capture the gleam in the eye and the thrill of youth. He can't do it, quite, but nearly always tries.

One day, this fishing grandson of mine was sitting on a dock catching perch and surrounded by adults who were not. It didn't do his growing ego any harm whatsoever. As I've said, he was badly bitten by the fishing bug, and on this occasion was nearly used for bait.

How would you react if you had been fishing alongside a six-and-half-year old child, had watched him catch half a dozen perch, and had gotten none yourself? Shall we say you might be restless? You might not say anything or do anything, but you would be conscious of the situation—right? Suppose that after he had caught another he commented to the surrounding adults in a child's treble, "I'll show you how to do it."

He was promptly admonished and lectured by his father. He was temporarily subdued somewhat by the strictures placed on him, but his ego wasn't in the slightest degree scratched, let alone damaged. Well, the weekend at the lake ended, school started, and the parents and grandparents rejoiced in an exuberant and well-mannered child.

The following spring he really started growing up. His father, deliberately and probably with malice aforethought, sentenced him to a life of frustration. He took him trout fishing in Vermont. He was warned that trout were not perch. He was told where to drop his worm and how to be patient when he felt a trout nibble; to wait a bit before setting the hook; to be sure the trout had his bait, etc. He hooked one, a seven incher, and with a mighty heave it sailed through the air and fell on the bank—more parental instructions. Honestly, the deliberate selfishness of his father was appalling! Here was a swell kid being condemned to a life of greater and greater frustration. It was carefully explained that he was lucky the trout fell off on shore and not in the water.

So they both headed downstream. Papa went ahead and the little fellow covered the water behind like the demon he was. Then a shout, "Daddy, look!" and louder and louder again, "Daddy, look!" Pop came running. Here was a really blissful boy. Hanging on the end of his line and swinging in the breezes of nature and youthful lungs, flipping its tail and bouncing up and down with the boy, was an eleven inch Brookie! This one had swallowed the hook half its length.

Pop had to extricate the hook, and once done and the trout duly presented to its rightful owner, the music started.

"I caught two trout." "I know this." "I know that." "I always catch fish—I know how." "I am the greatest." "I am," ad infinitum.

Now my son-in-law is a pretty good fisherman. He's also a pretty good parent. I learned for the first time that he also had a good memory and a conscience. He recalled previous braggadocio and he probably guessed that grandpa would blame any lack of fishing sportsmanship on him and not on the boy. I would have, too!

So down they sat in a good "father and son" conversation. It must have been a humdinger! Humility was emphasized. Luck was touched on heartily. Good manners and sportsmanship were the subject of a major conference. Dale Carnegie was probably brought in as suggested reading, and it was pointed out that the Good Lord had something to do with what happened to us mortals.

Now my second grandson is a smart kid and he has proven he can listen. He is also persistent and equipped with a memory. That evening, when it came time to go to bed, the prayers ran about as follows:

Now I lay me down to sleep
And pray the Lord my soul to keep,

. . . .

God bless Mummy and Daddy
And all my brothers,

. . . .

Thank you, God, for helping me catch

ABROAD

Two trout today,
And—God———
Shall we call it fifty-fifty?

The Measure of the Fish
or
Bombs Away

SOME FISHERMEN have wives. My wife does not fish. My wife doesn't want to be around when I fish. Some fishermen have such wives. She doesn't want to see, admire, hear about, smell or even eat a trout. We'd been married a year when for the first (and last) time I took her fishing. It was a great mistake. She agrees, but that is another story. This situation sometimes has advantages—not always, just sometimes.

Think of how you'd feel if your wife fished and you were telling yarns about stalking and landing a large, wild fish—when friend wife pipes up with the observation that she saw you trailing the hatchery truck! Think how differently you'd feel when you arrived back at the car thoroughly soaked and instead of saying, "You poor dear, you must be chilled to the bone, here, take this (5 ounces of good bourbon)," she said, "You dumb ox, I told you that ledge slid off into deep water, and furthermore, that you needed more hobs!" The very fact we don't have to confess our stupidity can be comforting. If she knew and said nothing, we'd pray she said something we could disagree with!

Think up a few more for yourself. My wife is a wonderful woman. She doesn't fish. I am confident that her avoidance of the art will not be diminished by this yarn, which was made possible solely because non-fishing wives must have a motherly instinct for their little boys, or a desire to get the brats out of their hair periodically.

At any rate, "the boss" and I were touring the Gaspe Peninsula and I'd sneaked a rod (or two) into the car. I was proceeding with care. For over a week I'd only fished half a day. We had duly admired everything we'd seen in this beautiful land and settled for a day at a little pension in the center of the peninsula. With the wonderful September air I slept late. We enjoyed a placid breakfast. I lingered for another cup of coffee and a cigarette so that the world's problems could be settled in an orderly manner.

These problems were never settled. Others, as is so often the case, were in the making. In fact, I never really started, for friend wife came back before my cigarette was finished and bomb shell number one splashed right into the coffee. "Did you notice the two old girls at the corner table?"

"No."

"There's a lake here. They're school teachers from Cleveland. They've never fished for trout before—and they've got the last boat and the last guide."

"Oh."

"Didn't you want to fish?"

"Yes, dear. Thank you."

She disappeared as fast as she had appeared.

Actually, that was pretty good detective work and more speedily accomplished than by a visit to the proprietor of the local sporting goods store, and there was no expense for unneeded tackle. The precise situation was succinctly stated.

It lubricated my fishing glands. Could the gals swim? Were the worms tied to the reels? Did they understand the guide in French? If I were a guide what would I do?—much too drastic! Beginners luck? Oh no! And lastly, why had my wife tried to get me fishing in a lake with mid-day approaching? Now these were things worth pondering. One could even conjure up some more intriguing challenges than the affairs of the world.

I had reached only one solid conclusion. The world was in one hell of a mess by eleven fifty-four, when my wife flew in bombshell number two.

"Look, they're back. They didn't catch anything and they said you could have the boat and guide 'til 2:30 if he was agreeable. He's getting sandwiches for two and will be ready at 12:15." Later I paid him willingly, and I suspect, also!

Some of my morning's musings were confirmed, but I never did find out why she shoved me off like a spoiled brat. The official statement was that I was too damned disagreeable to have around. Maybe such musings aren't exactly fruitless!

We rowed around in the manner of 'l'habitant' and in the brightest part of the day caught and released a few mediocre trout. I had worked, and of course shared cigarettes with the guide and tried to improve my French. The boat and the fly drifted. The fly sank and the boat didn't. A glance at my wrist watch coincided perfectly with the car horn and then the call, "Did you catch any fish?"

"Yes dear, on my way," I called.

"C'est necessaire chez nous."

"Oui, m'sieur," grinned the guide.

I picked up the rod and dropped the cigarette overboard. My guide picked up the oars and kept his. I reeled 'til the line stopped. Suddenly the rod bent—

"Sacre bleu! Un grand poisson!"

"Sacre Blue—NUTS—this is the hell of a trout!"

All good fish deserve conversation and a personal appellation while being played. This was Joshua—and we fought the Battle of Jericho! I blew the trumpet; the guide organized the cheers and advice section; my wife screamed questions that were never heard! French profanity flew in every direction and in due course we got the fish inboard, without a man overboard. I landed it in front of my spouse. She even asked to see it. Whether she said, "Mission accomplished," I do not know. My friend, the guide, and I speculated on its weight and he was very well paid indeed. My wife, after some nose tilting grimaces, suggested I show it to the teachers. She must have been thinking of grandchildren's education. The guide agreed with me, it should be weighed. "C'est magnifique!"

We arrived at the pension. The girls were waiting. The guide and I sought the chef with his scales, trailed by three females. This official let his sardonic gaze fall on my perfectly formed and colored prize—irreverently tossed it on the scales and said, "Too-an-haf." My English burst forth in words not generally taught in the Cleveland schools. The Lord of the Dietary merely shrugged his shoulders—oh so expressively—moved his body slightly so I could see, and there, sure enough, exactly on the nose—"Too-an-haf"!

Not to be outdone by his savoir faire, I directed that he cook my darling for the two school teachers, both of whom were making noises that were not even comprehended. My wife was humming to herself and saying nothing. Neither were the guide and I—just two weak, silent men. You could see, feel, and hear his visions of more money going up the flue!

I had a good drink and some troubled slumber. That evening the fish was served at the dinner table in the corner, garnished with oranges, lemons, and hay of various kinds. For all I knew, it may have had a potato in its mouth. Two-thirds was left on the platter when I left the dining room and trudged with furrowed brow into the library.

Bomb number three got me right between the eyes! Holy smoke! There on the wall were mounted numerous respectable trout—each carefully labled 3 lb. 7 oz., 4 lbs. 1 oz., 2 lbs. 15 oz —all, yes ALL, smaller than my fish! What the hell! Mine was but to reason why. Bravely I rushed for the kitchen. People fell by the wayside. Pots and pans and all culinary equipment jounced from the walls, ceilings, and floors. Bigelow also was unhinged! The chef was an imperturbable - - - - - -! He was finishing my fish! He handed me the scales. He might have shoved them down my throat!! Holy sufferin' Catfish! They were in kilograms—2½ kg. equals exactly 5½ honest pounds of perfect Salvelinus Fontinalis!

I'm really glad my wife doesn't fish. If she did, this would not have happened, and furthermore, she might be provoked into questioning this kilogram stuff.

The Tombstone Touch

A FEW YEARS BACK my wife and I took off for Scandinavia. There wasn't enough time in six weeks to cover even a tiny fraction of their gorgeous water. There never is. However, give me credit for carrying one eight-and-one-fourth-foot, two-piece rod back and forth across the Atlantic, up and down mountains, in and out of buses, railroad trains, airlines, museums, art exhibits and all the places where tourists are shuttled. Both the rod and I survived and as I have clasped its beautiful four ounces to my bosom during the intervening years, I have never failed to think of the future and my tombstone. It's thrilling!

My wife has my number completely. After touring Bergen, Norway, she shepherded me to a little inn where trout fishermen were said to relax. We took the train and I took the seat nearest the window. I didn't want that rod hurt so kept it in my hand between the window and me. My wife contended with traffic in the aisle.

We arrived in the evening. It wasn't the best season for brownies as the sea-run fish had not come in as yet. But looking around the lodge and talking to mine host briefly, I could see that this was what I'd wanted. Even with only three Norwegians and three Cockneys, they looked the way they should look—right. It was the first time I'd fished in Europe and I was very conscious of the obligation of helping our country's image both as a citizen and a sportsman. So many unfortunate people reach our own streams, I really dreaded leaving any bad taste for future Americans. Our State Department has multitudinous problems as it is. Also, I wanted to fish again.

Dinner was delicious, and afterwards the late evening gave the barefoot banker from the States the perfect opportunity to make the diplomatic approach to the following day's activity. I happened to notice that the other stray men were admiring the beautiful country and I did likewise. My accent gave away my country, and somehow or other the subject of fishing came up. The Norwegians all spoke English, so I've forgotten whether they or our English brethren brought up fishing. Also, they were all agreed.

The conversation couldn't possibly have been friendlier or, for that matter, less subtle. It reminded me of how our ministers, doctors, lawyers, bankers, and friends all tell us to think of the future. Our parents told us the same thing—even as we tell our children and grandchildren. Following this good advice is another matter and only you and I know how much application we've given to such irrefutable logic. Some fellow fishermen tell us to "watch your back cast." Do you always do so?

It developed that there was very little dry fly fishing in this area and that I should not be hampered mentally by my experience elsewhere. Being the barefoot banker, I asked why and was told far more politely than I write here that "if I really knew anything about trout, the water was much too high to even consider such a thing." "Furthermore, it's the wrong season."

Since this experience I have been giving the matter increasing attention, largely because of fellow fishermen from foreign lands. I've retired from banking. I've drawn my will (with legal advice, of course). I see my doctor regularly and sometimes follow his advice. I contribute regularly to my church, but fundamentally remain a weekend fisherman. My friends get

fewer so there is less advice to heed and now I have planned my tombstone.

I asked about their tackle with due humility and of course brought out my own after sufficient urging: one rod, a very few flies, a vest and waders. The type of waders was a curiosity, the vest was admired and the rod and flies—well, nothing was said directly, but their diplomacy was also artful. I was offered the loan of at least six rods and an appropriate number of flies. Putting on a good imitation of the State Department in action,

I assured my new friends that I felt my misfortune should be mine and not theirs. For the moment a diplomatic incident was avoided.

Darkness came at last. We were excused from each other and I went to bed with a heavy and stubborn heart. Should I follow all this advice? Morning broke and each of my friends was able to get on the stream before I finished breakfast. I had no chance to ask for any further pearls of wisdom. It was quite a problem. Bankers are sensitive, and I was conscious of my responsibilities away from home and the State Department's possible need of a thoughtful amateur ambassador. Perhaps it would ease world tension if I deliberately used my own approach and in due course admired their great perspicacity.

Mine host solved one problem. He delivered me unto a farmer possessed of a boat and located on a wide stretch of the river. The good farmer was really a stout fellow. His oars were made from four-by-fours. They seemed as long as sculls. One end of each had a whittled handle and the other end was shaped down by hand to a narrow blade. He was stout, and handled them like toys.

He spoke no English but could look it. In due course I persuaded him, by looking Norwegian, to let me off on an island, the head of which lay between two long fast runs where the river rushed down to our water. He deserved his rest on his timbers; I hope I deserved what I got. The fishing was good and challenging, both sides of the island: wading tricky enough to be enjoyable; a short swift float; a quick strike; a good fish. It was a gorgeous day and I loved every minute, in spite of the fact "the water was much too high, the flies "were no good" and my rod, well—I wouldn't even consider lending it to the State Department.

In due course we drifted his boat back to the car and parted the friendliest of friends in looks—words in English, Norwegian and mixtures thereof—and in deeds.

Back at the inn, my diplomatic friends were waiting with their fish laid out on boards for inspection. No one greeted me as I walked up the roadway. All eyes looked alternately at me and then the fish.

To this day I am grateful that my rod was still strung up and that my fly was still on the leader. I propped it carefully against something and composed my soul. My waders came off with the usual effort. My wife brought my loafers and got gruff answers for her pains. Before I picked up my creel, I lit a cigarette and then took my fish one by one and laid them below each catch. Unfortunately I couldn't quite match my six friends—I had one more fish than their collective catch!

During a sleepless night spent reflecting on my sins, I had composed the following for my tombstone:

Here lies Bigelow
Dead as a smelt
With the State Department
Under his belt!

Chile

I STILL DON'T BELIEVE IT. No trout fishing can be that good! Nothing like this has ever happened to me. I have simply got to go back to find out if it is so. Somehow or other, the more I think of it, the more I believe it ain't so, but I can't be sure.

A civic endeavor took me to South America. It seemed foolish being down there not to take a look at the trout streams of southern Chile. This was one of the best decisions I ever made. I arrived by air at Osorno on October 10th. This is the equivalent to April 10th north of the Equator. April 10th in Connecticut can be anything, cold, high water, and anything else. October 10th in southern Chile seems to work the same way.

Actually I had a remarkable guide, Alfred Heusser, for nine days. We traveled around and fished a different stream practically every day. We did not fish the lakes. In all that time I was never without fish for food or excitement, and in all that time I never caught a fish under one pound!

When you go to a country totally different from your own, it certainly pays to look at the terrain itself. Here was a fisherman's dream as to beauty. The water is crystal clear and heavy! There are white-capped mountains; beautiful twisting streams deep pools; fast water and mostly pretty large and heavy at that! There are very few people fishing. I recall only once or twice that we saw anybody else. There are rolling hills and volcanic outcroppings. The flowers are stunning and a lot of them the same as our own. Apparently the flowers grow eighteen months each year. No snakes, and, I am told, even in warmer weather practically no bugs. It was interesting to me personally that much of the country had been logged. The eucalyptus trees seem to have taken over the landscape, just as the Rainbows and Browns have taken over the streams.

These fish apparently live largely on pancora, which is a crazy bug that lives in the water, somewhat like a crawfish and shaped like a scarab. They seem to come in an assortment of sizes to fit the trout. The trout love them, and if the trout were happy so was I.

To go back to the country, it is quite a thrill to bounce along fast, clear water and look ahead on the stream and see a live volcano with smoke coming out the top and then have Alfred tell you if you wanted to, you could ski there that afternoon.

So you say the country is fine, but what about the fish and how do you do it? Well, it only makes sense to me that when you go to a new country, at least until you get the lay of the land, you see how the people fish who live there. This was a new one on me and most of the time I had to follow it because it seemed the only practical way. The Indians don't speak English and probably their way is the only sensible one to them. That's another reason I want to go back—to find out whether it is the only practical way, because I happen to like the dry fly *upstream.*

What you do is to get yourself a boat and an Indian that is good with the oars. He sits up front and rows continuously upstream. You sit in the stern fishing downstream, which is the way to fish, with big streamers. In spite of how the Indian rows upstream, the boat goes downstream! His skill comes in taking you through the fast water and those spots where HE thinks you may find fish. If you speak Spanish it won't help as he speaks only Mapuche which doesn't help much. The result is that at the start, you are apt to do pretty much as you are told. It's different, but, when those fish hit you know it!

I recall catching a twelve pound Rainbow in Lake Pond O'reille, Idaho—it was twenty six inches long and twenty six inches around! These fish in Chile are not built with either Pond O'reille or Bigelow proportions. They are lean, tough and determined. The big ones I thought, inexperienced as I am, have a great urge to go like a bat out of hell straight upstream!

Joking aside, I had only a few six pound test leaders, an awful lot of four pound tests were broken and some of the sixes. I had just one eight pound test, and that I found in time to use the last two days only. Next January or February I shall have different equipment!

We started out at a sensible hour—say about nine o'clock, throwing back the small fish, which included those of three or more pounds, unless we wanted food for lunch, and kept the larger ones for smoking. On every trip we took some bread, some beer, some salt and, absolutely always, plenty of the delicious Chilean white wine. Every day we had broiled trout. Each lunch was eaten with white wine. Every day after lunch we would lie down for half an hour to an hour's siesta on the bank. It was a hard life!

About this time, some cynical readers would be apt to say, "Well, Bigelow is talking about Paradise, but what about the fish?" Let me say this, I took two Orvis rods, one 4¼- and one 2-ounce. Most of my leaders, as I have already told you, were four pound, some six and one, joy to my heart, eight pound test. As I also have told you, I broke a lot of the fours on big fish. Let me add that part of this was probably my fault. I am not accustomed to throwing back two and three and four pound trout. I was told I held them too tight. That's the trouble with having nerves, but I defy any normal weekend fisherman not to find that he has nerves too. I have great resolves to take nerve tonic with me if I make the trip again. Incidently, to answer another criticism, I love that two ounce rod and prefer to fish with it. As a matter of fact, both there and in Canada, I have caught six pound fish with it. Lee Wulff is said to have caught fish in the twenty pound category with this identical rod. He is a much, much better fisherman than I ever thought of being. Whether or not he loves the rod I do not know, but, regardless, I do.

As I have said earlier, I once caught a twelve pound Rainbow. As I also observed at the start of this yarn, my abnormal disposition is to see what the natives do, but my normal stubborn disposition makes me keep on trying what I am accustomed to. The question of judgment brings the thrill of enjoyment, and the doubt remaining provides for the next trip.

Came the last day. We fished a medium- to small-size river, the Liucura out of Pucon. I had both rods strung up and where I could, fished the lighter fellow with a dry fly and the bigger rod with a big streamer.

I have just looked at my fishing license, which cost me twenty cents and entitled me to something like twenty fish "for each excursion." The following two stories are worth twenty cents to me. If I was starving, I might make more than one excursion a day. I am sure it has been done. But to get back to the fish stories, the first is one with the big 4 ¼-ounce rod and about the fish that got away. The second is about three fish that did not get away from me or my two-ounce rod.

Here is the first. We were rowing upstream and going downstream. I felt as if there was some scum or weight on my line. I started to strip it in and drop it in front of me in the boat. My Indian drew over to the side of the stream which was about two hundred feet wide at that point, and in which there was a real whirlpool at least one hundred feet across. He switched directions in view of the whirlpool so that he was rowing downstream and barely holding his own upstream. I stripped in my thirty yards of tapered line, dropping it between my legs in

the bottom of the boat and watching to see when I got to the leader. As the top of the leader came out of the water, I saw the fish strike and knew that this one was bigger than any of the others I had lost. I struck lightly and worried about letting those thirty yards out without getting tangled. I did accomplish at least this. When I came to the one hundred yards of backing, I struck hard. All hell, or all Chile, seemed to break loose at once. That fish went upstream so fast that I cut three fingers on the backing. I couldn't hold it! The backing disappeared until I felt a bump when it hit the reel spool. The line went slack.

My Indian laughed and I laughed, with tears in between. So I started to pick up my line and had it in maybe half way when the boatman yelled again. I had managed to get it all tied up on the oarlocks. He took four or five minutes to get it loose. I had gotten in most of the backing when he yelled again. There was my line going around and around the whirlpool! The fish was still on! Evidently, when the line hit the reel spool, one hundred and thirty yards upstream, the fish changed his little mind and came down. This time I was really scared! A two-ounce rod, a six pound test leader, three cut fingers and a very badly shaken soul, if any. I knew I could do no horsing job, so I kept on as much pressure as I dared (remembering broken leaders) for about five minutes. I thoroughly appreciate what Popeye the Sailor would say, but I had no spinach. In due course the hook fell out again, probably because of that reel spool bump.

No, I can't tell you how much that fish weighed. I didn't catch him. I saw him just once! I can't believe for a minute he was less than fifteen pounds and my guess is in the neighborhood of twenty. He got away and will undoubtedly survive. Maybe I will too. At least I didn't lose a sinking line on this fellow as I did on an earlier big fish.

Now if a person has fished for many years, he knows that there are fish that are caught as well as those that get away. So the second story follows:

After lunch we came to water which I could fish with a dry fly. My Indian and I had had some wine together and I think he had learned fifteen words of English. Bless him, when I waved my arms he knew what I meant, and didn't think I was completely nuts. This situation, my friends, makes a world of difference. If I get to Chile again, I am going to locate this man, period!

At any rate, I had some dry fly bivisibles on No. 6 hooks. My boatman was a super intelligent fellow. He knew this was the last day. His heart also had been well softened. So, in due course we put the rod back in its case. We also weighed two Rainbows and one Brown. Collectively they weighed fourteen pounds and eleven ounces. All were caught on one dry fly with a two-ounce rod. When we parted, my Indian friend got my six remaining large dry flies, my four remaining six-pound test leaders, and my sole and only eight-pound salmon leader. These made him happy, also me.

Back at the hotel, a chauffeur took my picture holding these three fish. I very carefully held them beside me and not out front. The result showed me in the sunlight and the fish in the dark. I still don't believe this trip!

The Test

AS AN IMMATURE AMATEUR, aged 68, I couldn't know less about fishing in England. A two-hour experience there and fifty-odd years here, however, leave many feelings in depth. I can't help but think of the beautiful approaches, gentle hills, narrow lanes, hedgerows, thatched roofs and the green grass of England. The whole picture seemed to lead to calm contentment and an almost holy desire to have the great of past centuries looking over one's shoulder, if not with approval at least with understanding acceptance. This privilege should be preserved for mature and experienced men who can, partially at least, understand and feel. One meat hunter would make another parasite shudder.

That portion of the Test which I fished was different from most of the fishing I've done in the United States. There's only one other stream I've fished here that seems comparable. The Brule in Wisconsin seems to have similar water flow, steady and inevitable. The Brule is spring fed and the Test is an underground river which comes up for air. Both in consequence have little variation in water level. The banks of the Test had paths from which you fished. The Brule is best fished from canoes. It's a puzzle to find the slope in the land to make them flow at their four or five miles per hour. There are also the patches of weed in the water. Both have dignity, a great historic past, and a serenity of their own. Izaak Walton wrote as few men have. It's perhaps a sacrilege for me to write of it all, except that these two loves were love at first sight. I regret other trips to England without a rod or an invitation much more than a little. I can't imagine living in England without spending more time fishing.

Let's go back to the stream. Prudence dictated a careful approach. This seemed natural and was, of course, necessary. Looking at the stream from above, I was immediately struck with the alternating patches of white chalk and green weed.

My fishing started, as always, with a Gray Fox Variant. Although there was an occasional reaction, it was obvious there was no enthusiasm. A guide had been obtained for a friend and myself. As my friend had little experience, he received most of the guide's attention. This was fine, for I was drinking in everything anyway. I did get a chance to show the guide my flies and he chose a Blue Dun, which, I say with pride, had natural hackles. I'm sure Izaak's had natural hackles also. This got attention, so I continued my efforts.

I'd been fishing the banks and had nothing of note and never anything from the bank from which I cast. I intensified my care and regretted my weight. I did fish slowly and in due course saw a good fish rise. The significance of "fishing the rise" really sank in for the first time. All of us have fished individual rises for particular fish. Most of our time, however, it has been for an individual fish, and not as a matter of procedure. This is what was to pay off. A few careful steps forward and the light permitted me to see a big fish rise, take a natural, and disappear.

Study showed that as a fly came over a white patch above, the fish rose from the weed and took the naturals above it at the juncture of chalk and grass. He then disappeared into the grass. The idea of "fishing the rise" in this water was beginning to get through.

My first cast was too short. The float only covered about half the water above the chalk. The fish rose, turned, and went down, no doubt saying to himself, "More flies will be along shortly." He was comfortable where he was. The next cast was all right as to distance, but the leader fell badly and I don't blame his majesty. There was a bit of a rest, another short cast, another rise, another turn, and, no doubt, additional comment on the inevitable future of better behaved flies. Fish can teach us all sorts of things, including patience, but they can't control our nerves. The next cast was what all its predecessors should have been, but I wasn't. I struck too hard. The fish was on briefly, but both won his point and shook mine. There was no sense in lingering longer here.

Thereafter I "fished the rise" and tried to place my fly as experience dictated. My control returned and I felt replete with calm appreciation of the fish, the fishing and, partially at least, with myself. I kept one fish for my hostess, which came to a bit over two pounds. When presented, there was a further gracious reward, a glass of Dry Sack Sherry. This had never happened to me before. Like a dry fly and a chalk stream in England, it has great virtue.

My few remaining Blue Duns, with natural hackle, and some Gray Fox Variants were left with my hostess. Like my thanks, they were inadequate for two hours satiate with pleasure. I was even told that my approach was correct.

Returning home, I had to re-read *The Compleat Angler.* Obviously I can't write as he did, but I hope I can convey some small share of his appreciation. I also re-read another book which was only discovered in 1955. The author's name has been lost. It was written in 1577, well before Izaak Walton. It was reprinted by the Princeton University Press. Izaak obviously knew the book for some passages are identical.

If you have gotten anything whatsoever out of this story, you should read both books, see what you can arrange in England, hock the family jewels and go. England, the water and the trout have been there a long time, but you don't have forever.

Fecundity

WHEN YOU MENTION British Columbia, some people think that it is in South America or Africa or Asia. It ain't. On my first trip to Western Canada (British Columbia) it was my good fortune to float my first fly on the Campbell River on Vancouver Island. It was also my very good fortune to meet on the stream a thoroughly competent fish and game editor from Vancouver. At the time of that first trip through our own Northwest as well as Canada, I was in my low fifties. I said then and have repeatedly reiterated, "If I had been thirty years younger I would never have come back."

My friend tried my Orvis rod as he had never fished with one before. While doing so, I commented, "This is a big country isn't it." He stopped casting, turned to me and said, "You don't realize how big. All of New England could fit comfortably into British Columbia, also, you could get seven New York States in here with room to spare."

"Is this the biggest Province?"

"Heavens no, there are several larger."

He was right. We in the East don't grasp these things until we get there. We have all heard about the Columbia River and its Grand Coulee Dam and its Salmon, in and out of the can. Those who have been to Jackson Hole, where the Snake River starts its big brawling life, those who have read the Lewis and Clark diaries know that this great river loses itself in the Columbia.

ABROAD

Probably comparatively few people realize that the Columbia starts in British Columbia and crosses into the U.S.A. Still fewer realize that its headwaters are only about forty or fifty miles away from another river of the same magnitude—the Fraser. The Fraser enters the ocean at Vancouver only about two hundred miles north of the mouth of the Columbia, which separates Washington and Oregon. It is a real he-man river. It has everything. It is big and it's as tough as they come. There is a long section where no boat is permitted for reasons of safety. Hundreds died here in the early exploration and settlement of the country. Its history is just as vivid as much of our own. Its economic importance, past, present and future is enormous. Much of the huge Province of British Columbia looks for parentage to the Fraser. It is georgeous, deceitful, treacherous, life-giving and fickle. Driving up the banks of the river would humble any dictator and even from the train window both fascinates and appalls. Some of our eastern rivers, beautiful as all good rivers are, make me think in comparison that someone forgot to shut off the faucet. If you want real grasp of the history, see if you can locate *The Fraser* by Bruce Hutchinson. It is part of The Rivers of America books and was published in 1950 by Clarke Irwin & Co. of Toronto. You will end up by visiting the country to see for yourself; to fish some of the unknown spots, to drink in many kinds of beauty, and perhaps to wish that you too had gone there as a young man.

The Fraser is shaped like a worn fish hook made of soft material. The eye is in Vancouver and extends 125 miles up to Lytton, where it is joined by the Thompson River and then goes on north to form the hook.

The Thompson is no mean stream with its own terrors and history and it, too, disappears in the Fraser.

My daughter, her husband, and at least two of their sons lived in Kamloops, about 100 miles northeast of Lytton, on the Thompson River four or five years. Some fishermen know it as the home of the Kamloops Trout (Rainbow). It is my impression that Lake Pend Oreille, New Zealand, Chile plus a few lesser spots were stocked originally with Kamloops Rainbows. To most of my friends, it was an unheard of spot, located somewhere between Tierra del Fuego and Alaska. This is one of the continent's or world's great trout centers and it is not completely spoiled as yet. There's too much of it.

That doesn't mean you always get trout. I recall one trip with the best guide I could get. We both fished together. He was good! For ten days we fished as hard as I was able, nearly wrecked the car daily and walked ten times too much! He got one fish and I got exactly none. That doesn't mean we didn't see them. Many times we saw hundreds spawning by the shores of lakes. I have bent low at times but I have never gone jigging. Three years later I fished without a guide. Fish caught daily averaged three or four pounds. It wasn't the guide it was the fish, and only the fish. Bigelow claims no credit.

When I talk about this country, the fool hens and other birds, the monumental fecundity of fish and game, the land itself and the absence of people, the old banker gets starry-eyed. I wish I knew enough about the other critters to write about them. I'm supposed to be sticking to trout, and it's possible I don't know enough about them either.

This is the story of one day only, when it seemed to me the trout herded salmon smolt the way a sheepdog herds sheep. As this story involves Sockeye Salmon as well as Kamloop Trout, let's take a background look at them also. Their life cycle is fantastic and lasts just four years. The mature fish come into Vancouver Sound in the Spring where they multiply their weight and strength by feasting on herring. When they start upstream in the fall to spawn and die, they have the strength to fight their way through water which has killed hundreds of men going downstream.

As they near their spawning grounds, the bodies of the males turn red, the females are paler. In consequence, in some spots and at some times the river looks red. At this stage of the game they are much more satisfactory food for bears than for humans. They also do strange things. It is known, for instance, that year after year in one place they come up the right bank to a certain point and then cross diagonally to the left bank. A fisherman wading can be and has been knocked over by a great run of salmon coming upstream.

In the spring the young hatch in fresh water streams and move to the lakes to live and eat and grow. When they reach their second spring and have attained a few inches, they start their long journey downstream to the sea.

It was at this stage that my son-in-law took me some forty miles up the Thompson River east of Kamloops to where the Little River enters Little Shuswap Lake. None of these waters are little by my standards. The water was wide, deep and strong. Boats were necessary and motors highly desirable.

We hired a boat and rigged our rods with big streamers. My son-in-law who has brains was handling the engine. As we idled out into the water, suddenly his voice said, "Now!" For about ten minutes the water was alive with rising fish, hundreds of them anywhere from one to ten pounds, maybe more! Some we hooked, some were lost, sometimes we swore. Then he said, "It's over, we'll wait awhile." We did and in due course it happened all over again.

It is time for questions. The reason for the streamers was that masses of salmon smolt went downstream from time to time. The reason for the rising fish was the smolt; the Kamloop Trout knew another batch would come later. This accounted for the periods of mayhem.

These trout got their bellies full in spurts by surrounding the smolt as no greeting committee ever did the visiting firemen. They had to have some time for digestion. The trout really were sheepdogs for the smolt. The only reason that so many lambs got away was that they were so myriad in number.

Study the books in advance. Go and see it. You will dream all night, remember always, and never regret.

OTHER FISH

Other Fish—A Postscript

HOW POSSIBLY could any thoughtful trout fisherman know how superior trout are to other fish if he did not sometimes try the other fish? The answer is that the brainy trout fishermen all know this. They don't object to other people fishing in any way they want for any other fish. In the great democracy in which we live that is the right of all who wish to fish. It is also my right to prefer trout. Many are unjustly maligned as purists —men who don't ever recognize anything else than their own preference. Fortunately I think these men are growing fewer as both their horizons and their beams broaden. I hope so.

On the other hand, a trout fisherman fishing for other fish can also overdo it. He can have another trip and, like the boy with another drink, remember it not with joy but with sorrow. All of which prompts me, in this description of five other fish, to tell first of the one I remember with both joy and sorrow.

Smelt

THERE IS THE OLD CHESTNUT of the fisherman who caught two fish. When he arrived home he had three—two mackerel and one smelt.

Boston Harbor is a big body of water. Many ships, tugs, yachts, scows and dories rush madly back and forth across its waters. This is the story of fishing one day with two friends who owned a boat of sorts. It floated in a way all its own. If you didn't care how you slept, it could sleep three men.

We went smelt fishing. The stormy winds did blow and three poor sailors, clinging to their rods, didn't care what happened down below. Rudder and rudder is what I got. I didn't care if anyone shot the sun but felt differently about the ocean.

We got over thirty smelt, big ones, great big ones. Our hands got so cold we could no longer hold onto the boat and rod at the same time. We went below. Somebody had forgotten some provisions. Starboard? Nuts! I forgave them both. They had a quart and a half of gin and about an ounce and a half of vermouth.

We didn't want to spill a drop so we made a run to a quieter place. We had a delectible supper consisting of numerous gourmet smelt. They all disappeared well laced with gin. This also disappeared. We had a quiet restful night and we didn't give a damn whether the wind blew or some one ran us down.

OH, BOY
HIC!
WHEEE—
I'M A BOID!

Large-Mouth Bass

FOLLOWING THE BANK HOLIDAY, the economic pressure on many people persisted. In the center of Greenwich is a residential development inhabited largely by upper middle income people. They were hard hit. I recall one family that was literally being helped with food by the neighbors. Their only boy had been able to sell his bicycle but nobody wanted to buy a battered second hand canoe. He found that he could get fifty cents for paddling evening fishermen around a lake in the center of this development. I was among his regular customers and seemed always to find sandwiches for two.

The bank Executive Committee meetings were held at 4:30 and, as I knew it was a short one coming up, I made a date with this youngster to fish at 5:30. One of my directors loved fish. He was a wise gentleman. When we finished our meeting at five, I asked him if he wished some fish for dinner. The answer was yes.

"How many?"

"Four."

"How large?"

"Two or more pounds each."

"What time do you have supper?"

"Six thirty."

"Tell your wife not to cook anything else, I'll be there."

I arrived early, the fish were going mad. I kept three of

about three pounds each and one of about six. I must have put back a couple of dozen and I arrived at his home with four fish at 6:29. He said they tasted good but I don't believe he had the fun I did.

Great Northern Pike

DURING THE MIDDLE THIRTIES, four of us took a week the middle of June to go to Schermerhorn's Landing on the St. Lawrence River. We got a cabin and cooking utensils of sorts. Our first day was spent in cleaning the cabin. We hired rowboats and one day splurged and had one outboard. A quart of Scotch had somehow floated over from Canada.

One day I came upon a big circle of seaweed on the surface. At the time I was the only person I saw on the St. Lawrence that was fishing bass flies and a few bugs, including a hair mouse. I put on the hair mouse and cast it with an old-time combination fly and bait casting rod into the center of the circle. It was tickled the way I thought an imaginative mouse should be tickled. The great grandad of all Great Northern Pike took that mouse and kept going. I held on for dear life! I didn't leave the boat but the leader left the line.

There was only one thing to do. I took the car and drove over seventy miles that afternoon collecting all the hair mice I could find. There must have been thirty. I went back to the charmed circle and I didn't catch a fish, but I came home without any of the thirty mice. Sometimes the leader broke; sometimes the fish got off; sometimes the hook was straightened but as a fish took I just held on. I never had so much fun in one day's fishing or lost as many fish!

When we got back to the Bear Mountain Bridge, as treasurer

I had paid all the bills so divided up the cost of the entire trip, including groceries, ice, gas and boats. I think the whisky came free. The tax per each from door to door was $16.95.

Small-Mouth Bass

OVER FIFTY YEARS AGO, when I was sixteen, two of us floated down the Tippecanoe River in Indiana. We were looking for small-mouth bass. We took a canoe for two weeks in the days when railroads were helpful. The train deposited us at a crossroads, canoe and all. Bacon should be taken in the flitch and cut with a "dull edge." By connivance of some sort an "old man" all of twenty-five met us at the end of a week.

We started our canoe where the river was about fifteen feet wide and we fished only in bathing suits. The stream was generally wooded, ran through a lot of farm country and was loaded with small-mouths. I am told there are some still left. A tree across the stream was an excuse to rock the canoe over it, to get a swim ourselves, to lighten the canoe or to just plain watch what went on about us.

We were plug fishing and I remember days when we were skunked and had to live on pancakes and bacon. Boys can do that indefinitely. We finally captured one frog and surveyed a pool from a high bank above it. There must have been about thirty bass in that pool. We drew lots. I won the frog. A perfect cast made the whole bottom of the Tippecanoe River explode. The frog disappeared. Which fish got it we never found out. We never caught another frog. When the froth went downstream, there were the thirty contented bass in their same station with two discontented boys on the bluff.

That night, in my bathing trunks, when we came to make camp I stepped out backwards and my foot came down on the neck of a five-foot black snake who proceeded to coil himself all about my leg up above the knee. At sixteen you can enjoy such things but as the years pass, I have an occasional nightmare. My companion laughed and unwound it.

In due course we met the "old man" of twenty-five at another crossroads. We walked seven miles into "town" to meet his train at about six-thirty. He wanted to eat. We told him it was a seven mile walk to camp. He spotted a house near the railroad station which had "hotel" over the door. We walked over and were greeted by the owner. We asked about food and was told, "Supper's over, but if you want some simple food I guess you can have it."

"What have you got?"

"Well, I killed a steer last week. I could give you a good steak."

"Fine."

"There's always fresh corn in the garden."

"Let's have it!"

"The Mrs. baked pies yesterday."

"Wonderful."

The steak that came was half the size of the canoe. Man and wife made alternate trips to the garden for more corn. When we had all we thought we could stand, we were brought one pie each. There's nothing quite like rising to a challenge and nobody but sixteen year olds would meet such a challenge so well. We conquered!

Finally the "old man" said, "What do we owe you?" The proprietor said, "Would twenty-five cents apiece be too much?"

Atlantic Salmon

A FEW YEARS AGO I went after salmon on the Miramichi. The water was low; it was hot on shore and almost as hot in the water. Pattern cast we did both wading and from canoe. Neither produced any results whatsoever.

So I took my little two-ounce Orvis and went up a feeder stream for brook trout. We had to eat fish and I got eighteen in less than two hours. I was fishing dry with a size 14 Gray Fox Variant. Having short cut the mouth of the stream on the way up, I noticed on the way down that a great bunch, fifty at least, of salmon and grilse were congregating just off the mouth of this stream. I cast with the trout fly and got interest. Perseverance produced one grilse. This required thought. Dinner also brought endless discussion.

Early the next morning my son-in-law and I put on the same No. 14 Gray Fox Variant and took our stations on each side of the outlet. He discovered that if you bounced the fly along the surface in little six inch hops, you got action. The result was we each had our four fish by 8:30. We then noticed eight or ten people, including two game wardens, on the cabin porch above us. It was distinctly unorthodox but it was more fun than pattern casting all the rest of the week put together.

So you've come to the end of a book
By a banker, who may be a crook.
For as you read his trash
Banker B got your cash,
Friend—fishermen always are took!

B.S. by O.B.